ARL
ANIMAL RESCUE LEAGUE OF IOWA, INC.

# For the Love of RESCUE DOGS

## THE GUIDE TO SELECTING, TRAINING, AND CARING FOR YOUR DOG

Tom Colvin, Paula Sunday, and Mick McAuliffe

*For the Love of Rescue Dogs*

CompanionHouse Books™ is an imprint of Fox Chapel Publishers International Ltd.

Project Team
Vice President–Content: Christopher Reggio
Editor: Amy Deputato
Copy Editor: Colleen Dorsey
Design: Mary Ann Kahn
Index: Elizabeth Walker

ISBN 978-1-62187-189-7

The Cataloging-in-Publication Data is on file with the Library of Congress.

This book has been published with the intent to provide accurate and authoritative information in regard to the subject matter within. While every precaution has been taken in the preparation of this book, the author and publisher expressly disclaim any responsibility for any errors, omissions, or adverse effects arising from the use or application of the information contained herein. The techniques and suggestions are used at the reader's discretion and are not to be considered a substitute for veterinary care. If you suspect a medical problem, consult your veterinarian.

Fox Chapel Publishing
903 Square Street
Mount Joy, PA 17552

Fox Chapel Publishers International Ltd.
7 Danefield Road, Selsey (Chichester)
West Sussex PO20 9DA, U.K.

www.facebook.com/companionhousebooks

We are always looking for talented authors. To submit an idea, please send a brief inquiry to acquisitions@foxchapelpublishing.com.

Printed and bound in China
22 21 20 19    2 4 6 8 10 9 7 5 3 1

# Contents

# Introduction

In a perfect world, all pets would have places to call home with loving owners who provide for all of their needs. However, we know that there are many reasons why this isn't true today; pet overpopulation, lack of affordable pet-friendly housing, and lack of pet education and resources, among others, contribute to pet homelessness. For those pets that have never experienced the love of an owner or that, due to unforeseen circumstances, can't continue to live with their owners, animal shelters and rescues play a pivotal role.

When pets can't find safe, loving homes, shelters or rescues give them food, rest, and behavioral and medical care, and they work to find them the loving homes we wish for them. But adoption doesn't end when you take

↗ Shelters and rescues, like the Animal Rescue League of Iowa, help pets find safe, loving forever homes.

← Rescue dogs come in all sizes, breeds, and temperaments. Which one will you make that special connection with?

Dogs do speak, but only
to those who listen.
—Orham Pamuk

your new pet home. When you adopt, we want you to adopt for life, but we know that pet ownership can come with challenges. Throughout this book, you'll learn about house-training, manners training, introducing your new dog to other pets and to children, and much more. The advice in this book doesn't just help you teach your dog new things, it will strengthen your bond with your new pet and help him settle into his forever home with you.

—Tom Colvin, Executive Director,
Animal Rescue League of Iowa, Inc.

# 1 From the Shelter's Perspective

In this book, you'll find guidance and advice built upon a lifetime of hands-on work with dogs of all ages in many environments. Each year, thousands of animals come into shelters and rescues. Among these animals are many beautiful, wonderful, sweet, and friendly dogs: young and old, big and little, purebred and mixed breed, and the list goes on. The knowledge we have gained working with these dogs and their owners will make both your dog's and your life better.

## What Most Potential Adopters Want

Many people arrive at the shelter with some idea of the type of dog they want to adopt. Some people think that they want to train a puppy. Some people worry that an older shelter dog is "ruined." Some want a dog that's not too big, or one that doesn't shed much. Some need a dog that's good with children all the time. Everyone wants a healthy dog that's easy to house-train.

The reality is that with positive training, dogs of all ages, from puppies to seniors, can be wonderful companions. Often, an adult shelter dog already has some training and could be the perfect dog for you. If you don't really want to house-train a puppy, you can avoid this issue altogether by adopting a house-trained adult dog. When thinking about

↑　**Adopters want a dog that will be a great companion.**

training and other important factors, such as children and dogs, health issues, a dog's size, and the care a dog needs, ask the shelter staff. They can help you make an informed and successful choice.

Sometimes, potential adopters fall for elderly, injured, or shy animals to "save" them. These matches often work out wonderfully with some TLC and coaching from a behavior expert. At the Animal Rescue League (ARL), we have made great strides

## Paula Says

For more than thirty years, my professional career has been tied to dogs. Dogs that need homes, training, grooming, socialization, or veterinary care. Most of my time has been spent in animal shelters. From my first day at a shelter, it was clear that pet owners and adopters need help. They need information from people who understand what they are going through. They need support to get through the stressful adjustment time after bringing their new pet home. They need answers to behavior questions. The tricky part is that most people don't realize that the time they need the help is *before* bringing the pet home.

with some pets, regardless of their special needs. Successful adopters call, e-mail, send cards, or stop by the shelter to show off their progress.

Other times, challenges can frustrate the "Good Samaritan" adopter. After a couple of months, the owner brings the special-needs pet back to the ARL for the very reason the person adopted the dog in the first place. We understand the frustration, but it saddens us. One good outcome, though, is that we can build a history for the pet, which will help us find him a new home that lasts.

## Creating the Bond

Throughout all our years of experience, we have learned that a dog stays in a home where there is a bond with the humans. All other factors considered, if there is no bond, the dog will likely be gone someday, often with no regrets—and maybe even relief—on the part of the humans. Even if the kids are attached but the adults are not, the dog is at risk. The bond can be based on attraction, love, and/or training, but the best predictor of success is training.

↓   **A shy pup can often flourish in a home with love, security, and positive training.**

# DOG TAILS

## Charlie Bear

Charlie Bear, a young male German Shepherd, was picked up by an animal control officer who immediately realized that Charlie's forelimb had been severely injured. The shelter veterinarian examined Charlie Bear, and, throughout the examination, X-rays, and tests, the dog demonstrated a great temperament and spirit. The decision was made to amputate the injured leg, and Charlie Bear continued to show his strength throughout his recuperative period. His endearing personality was obvious to all and especially to the wonderful family that adopted him.

So, how do you build a bond with a dog? Is it something chemical, like falling in love?

Dog lovers can recognize that instant attraction of "Oh my, who is that dog?" Sometimes it is love at first sight, and sometimes it is just an inquiry into the breed or why it looks the way it does.

What causes the connection? It could be our history with dogs, or it could be recognizing similarities to a dog we knew in the past. It could be a specific feature that catches our eye—big brown eyes, fuzzy ears, a wagging tail, or a certain coat color. This initial attraction is the beginning and sometimes the end. People will disregard a wonderful dog because they don't like something in his looks, but they often discover that their opinion changes dramatically after getting to know the dog.

What keeps a dog in a home for a lifetime? Attraction and love can keep a dog in his home for a lifetime, but sometimes they are not enough. A dog needs manners. Unruly behaviors, unreliable house-training, and even normal behaviors like digging, jumping, and chewing can frustrate families. Frustration usually sets in after about six months. Owners realize they do not have time to house-train, exercise, and

↑   **Positive, reward-based training helps build the dog-owner bond.**

supervise the new dog, and children really don't have any interest in a pet that jumps on them or chews on their stuff. Eventually, we don't like the dog we love. Even temporary frustrations can cause a total break in the bond. Often, owners wait too long to help their pet when a little training, supervision, management, and exercise could have taught good manners and kept the pet in his home. The outcome is completely different when owners realize that having a well-behaved dog begins with them and that communicating with their dog through training will create a bond that results in a lifelong home.

Why is training the best predictor of success in creating a lasting bond? We have learned that training affects the human-dog bond to the point where, excluding changes in an owner's life, it is extremely rare for our shelter to take in a dog who has been through any formal dog training classes. The commitment to participate, the practice to get proficient, the peer pressure in the class to demonstrate what you've been taught, and the satisfaction of having success with new behaviors at home really make a difference.

# DID YOU KNOW?

When people see a well-behaved dog, they often think, *I wish my dog acted like that.* Maybe they've been able to train their dog or puppy to sit, but they've become frustrated in trying to train any other behaviors. After watching someone else's dog sit, lie down, and do tricks on cue, owners are both amazed and dismayed. They don't believe their dog could learn anything like that. As a training-class instructor, it is no small joy for me to show owners how to help their dogs begin to understand behaviors that they want their dogs to perform.

## Training Starts Early

Research shows that puppies learn very quickly during their first sixteen weeks of life. If you adopt a young puppy, start him in puppy classes between eight and twelve weeks of age. In these classes, your puppy will learn basic manners and socialization. (See Chapter 3).

During these early weeks, a puppy's brain is particularly responsive. It is the time when puppies should become accustomed to gentle touch and positive experiences. Owners should introduce their pup to the outside world by supervising his interactions with children and adults and by gently introducing him to other pets and to different environments. Puppy classes are a key element in bonding and in teaching the manners needed to keep the puppy in his first home.

In contrast, when owners don't know how or don't take the time to train the basics, their puppy can become a dog that jumps on people, chews inappropriately, gets into garbage, pulls on his leash, barks excessively, or worse.

## What a Dog Needs

Dogs are straightforward creatures with simple, basic needs.
**Physical needs:** Play, food, exercise, housing/shelter, mental stimulation
**Emotional needs:** Communication, understanding

↑ Owners want a well-mannered dog at home and in public.

Knowing how important it is to train before fatigue sets in and before the bond is broken, the ARL encourages owners to call us so we can record a short history of their issues and discuss options for their specific situations. (Refer to Chapter 10 for advice on modifying problem behaviors.) It is our goal to help owners communicate with their dogs through training and keep the dogs in good homes for their entire lives. It is sad when we see a bond broken and a dog surrendered to the shelter to find a new home when good manners were just a few training sessions away. (See the Nothing in Life Is Free method of positive training in Chapter 8).

As much as we wish that all animals could stay in forever homes, we know that shelters will always be needed. Some animals are brought in as strays. Others are brought in when owners experience major life changes, such as illness, having to move to senior housing where pets are not allowed, a work schedule that doesn't allow time for the pet, allergies in the family, or becoming unable to afford a pet. Often for these families, giving up the pet is heartbreaking and traumatic. In these instances, wonderful pets become available for adoption.

## Important!

Be sure that your puppy is current on his vaccinations before taking him to a puppy class.

Many people who foster tend to foster the breed that they are most familiar with or attracted to. Many years ago, I decided to foster a Chow Chow puppy even though it wasn't a breed I was familiar with. I named her Fox and felt sure that after some handling and TLC, she would be able to go right into a new home with someone who understood Chows. I was right—Fox lived with us for fourteen years and taught me a lot about the breed's behavior and communication.

## Fostering

When a pet is surrendered and needs an interim home to get him ready for adoption, the pet is placed in foster care. Volunteers foster pets for what are intended to be short periods of time. However, sometimes the foster family falls in love with the pet and decides to adopt him themselves. The foster family also risks feeling responsibility and fear that the right home won't or can't be found for the dog when he is ready for adoption.

↑　If you adopt a puppy, you can begin easy lessons with him as soon as he comes home with you.

↑ Shelter volunteers start handling and socializing the puppies to prepare them for their new homes.

A potential foster must consider if he or she can take on a pet with special needs or a young litter of puppies that need time to grow up. Bless those people who can devote the time and care required in these instances, because it takes a lot, both physically and emotionally.

## Laws for Animals

The federal Animal Welfare Act, passed in 1966, requires breeders who have more than three breeding female dogs and who sell puppies to pet stores or puppy brokers to be licensed and inspected by the US Department of Agriculture (USDA). Unfortunately, the USDA is overburdened.

But you can help. Follow your city, state, and federal representatives and tell them that animal welfare legislation is extremely important to you. Contact your local animal shelter to find out other ways you can help.

# HAPPY ENDINGS

## Mia

Mia, a mixed breed about five and a half years old, was brought into the shelter by a farmer who told us, "She was dumped in my yard." Mia was full of ticks and *very* pregnant. She appeared to have lived in the country because "city noises" made her very nervous.

Karen volunteered to watch over Mia at the shelter until she had her eight healthy puppies. Karen then took Mia and her little family home with her until they were ready to find their new forever homes.

# FOR FOSTER DOGS

## Oksana

Shortly after passage of puppy mill legislation, a commercial breeder relinquished 300 dogs to a shelter. Oksana, a very pregnant Corgi, was one of these 300 "breeder" dogs.

Karen and the shelter watched over Oksana during her delivery. Then, through the foster-home program, Karen brought Oksana and her seven puppies home to care for them prior to adoption. Karen considered adopting one of the puppies, but she fell in love with Oksana and adopted her instead.

At first, Oksana did not like to be touched. She didn't know human contact. She would leave her bed only to eat and to go outside to potty. She had the habit of walking in small circles; perhaps that was the only space she was used to. Her entire life had been spent confined to a 3-foot by 3-foot (1 meter square) kennel.

Karen says that Oksana started to allow some petting after about four months, and after about a year and a half, she was still a little shy but very happy in her loving home.

# 2 Understanding Dog Behavior and Communication

**W**atching dogs gives us the opportunity to identify their emotions, such as fear, stress, anxiety, and love. Misunderstanding how dogs communicate causes humans to make many handling errors. We can make our dogs' lives happier and easier if we can begin to identify and interpret their language.

Try this quiz:

- True or false: A wagging tail on a dog always means that he is happy and friendly.
- True or false: A puppy with his mouth open, showing his teeth, is going to bite.
- True or false: An adult dog showing all of his teeth is going to bite.
- True or false: Children always understand that dogs can bite, so children won't try to take their dog's food or toys.

Hopefully you answered *false* to all of the questions. We need to evaluate the whole picture of the dog, not just the tail, mouth, ears, or other individual parts. Dogs communicate with their whole bodies, and every muscle has a role. We believe that dogs want us to understand their communication, but because it is so different than our own, we do not always get it right.

There are major differences between human and canine communication. Human communication is based on verbal language with some body language added for emphasis. Humans make direct eye contact, often prolonged. We face each other in greeting, approaching in a straight line, holding out our hands for a handshake or a hug.

↑　Signs of a friendly meeting are when dogs approach each other at a curve, heads slightly down and eyes averted.

Canine communication is based primarily on body language and uses very little vocalization. In a friendly approach to another dog, a dog's head is held down slightly, his tail wagging slowly from side to side, and his eyes to one side or the other but never making direct eye contact. A friendly approach also includes the two dogs sniffing each other's genitals, noses, and mouths for information about their sexes and who knows what else. That's only the beginning of the body language that goes on between two dogs. There are play bows, ear positions, tail positions, and facial expressions. Their mouths may be open or closed, and their bodies either loose and wagging or stiff with hackles up. The dogs may stand up on their toes, trying to look bigger, or they may slink in, eyes averted, maybe even rolling on their backs at first meeting.

Scent is a huge part of the greeting behavior. Even from a distance, you can see a dog air-sniffing to catch a scent of another dog in the area. Sight can be important, but scent is the key, followed by sight and then sound.

Dogs interpret information from other dogs through body language and facial expressions. Every muscle in a dog's face and head is used to communicate. The body language is measured in terms of millimeters of movement: a head turn to the right or left, lips tightened over the teeth, eyelids held still or tightened against the eyes. Even the muscles of the forehead and eyebrows make expressions that other dogs can read and interpret.

## For More Info...

Read *The Other End of the Leash* by Patricia McConnell for an interesting look at how dogs interpret human behavior.

## Body Language Signals

Dogs give us many signals. Signals are often combined and may be conflicting if the dog is stressed, frightened, or frustrated. Dogs use every muscle, turn, weight shift, paw lift, eye movement, and even breathing rate to communicate. Because this is a foreign language to us, we need to observe and identify so we can communicate with our own dogs. One reason humans love having dogs around is because of the relationships we have with them. They "listen" and want to be near us. When we begin to "listen" to them, too, our relationships become even more meaningful.

↑   Dogs sniff the air to get the scent of other dogs in the area.

↑   **Licking may be a calming behavior.**

## Licking

Licking happens so frequently that we often miss seeing it. Your dog may be using licking to talk to other dogs. It is very quick and often used in combination with other behaviors, like head turning. It can be a full nose lick or a flicking of the tongue, just touching the lips.

## Tail Wagging

Tail wagging is not a good singular signal of a dog's intent. A tail held high and wagging fast can mean that the dog is highly aroused, intense, or agitated. A low tail, wagging slowly, can mean that a dog is waiting to see what comes next. A still tail is always to be taken seriously, whether it is tucked under the body or standing straight out from the body. Movement is always better than stillness in canine language. And remember, no matter what the dog's tail is doing, take in the behavior of the whole dog.

## Yawning

Yawning seems to be contagious not only among humans but also among dogs. It acts as a stress reliever and should always be interpreted to mean that something is concerning the dog. Yawning back at him can actually help him decide not to worry.

↑ **Yawning acts as a stress reliever.**

## Head Turning/Turning Away

While it appears that a dog turning away is accidental or even random, a dog turns his head for a reason. If he turns his head away from you when you are talking to him, maybe you are being unclear, stern, or a bit scary. Your dog may turn his head just a bit or a complete 90 degrees. His goal is to calm you down and avoid conflict.

Observe your dog when a stranger approaches him straight on. He will always turn his head to the side. The person is being a bit rude, and your dog is being very polite. This is a great conflict-avoidance behavior for dogs. They use it often and for many reasons. When you see your dog turn his head, try to determine why.

If you are petting your dog on one side, and he turns his head away from you, he may not enjoy the petting. Try changing where you are petting him and see if he turns toward you.

## Play Bowing

The play bow is an invitation to another dog to play. Dogs use it with humans, other dogs, and even other species. You will notice the lowered front legs as the dog hops from side to side.

Dogs also use the play bow to avoid conflict and to calm fearful or nervous dogs. If you watch a group of dogs, and a new dog approaches, the group usually stands still until one of the dogs in the group does a play bow. Then, everyone calms down, and often there is a play/chase session. Sometimes the dogs just calmly walk away.

## Sniffing the Ground

Sniffing the ground is a signal that seems random until you start observing how purposefully dogs use it. Dogs do sniff a lot, because they want to know what dogs have been through the neighborhood. If your dog is approached by a person or another dog, he may lower his head to sniff, indicating that he is no threat, and his intent is to avoid any conflict or confrontation.

## Walking Slowly

Walking slowly is an interesting behavior to watch in a group of dogs. Sometimes, when the play gets too rough or too loud, or a new dog approaches, all dogs slow down into what appears to be slow motion. Sometimes you will see a young dog ignore the others and just slam around into the other dogs. He will probably get a growl, snap, or other

↑　When a dog turns his head away from you while petting, try petting a different place on his body and see if he relaxes.

correction from one of the adult dogs. This will help him concentrate and see what the others are doing. Dogs are great at learning to mimic other dogs, so it's likely that he will quickly slow down. Speed can be too arousing and confrontational.

Watch your dog as he approaches something novel, like a toad. Chances are, he will slow down and approach softly, evaluating whether it is a toy, food, or something dangerous.

Watch your own dog when you call him. If he is slow in responding, take a look at your body language as well as his. Does he start out quickly and then slow down, turn his head, or stop to sniff the ground? This can look like he is ignoring you on purpose, and it can be very frustrating. Can you help him come more quickly by turning your head or body to the side, yawning, using a softer, friendlier tone of voice, or moving slowly away from him?

## Freezing

Freezing is when a dog stops all motion and is totally still, usually only for a split second. Dogs use this behavior to communicate a warning. If a dog has a bone or something else valuable, and he freezes as you approach, he is trying to get you to go away. He will also use this with other dogs and pets in the household. Of course, children don't understand why the dog freezes. If the child continues to approach after a dog has signaled concern by freezing, he may start to escalate his communication to the obvious but unacceptable growling, snapping, and biting behaviors.

Fearful dogs use freezing to try to relieve conflict. It is often used in combination with other behaviors, such as slow motion, depending on the dog's communication efforts. It is an important behavior for humans to understand.

↑　Pip is ready to play, but Elle turns her head to say, "Not now."

↑　Sniffing the ground may seem random, but dogs use this action to avoid conflict or confrontation.

## Pawing

A dog may paw to try to get a human's attention. It is a behavior that is also used to appease a conflict if the human seems distressed or angry. We rarely see pawing used with other dogs, just with humans.

## Sitting with Rowdy Puppies

You will sometimes see an adult dog sit down with a rowdy or playful puppy in an attempt to calm the youngster. If that doesn't help, the adult may turn his back or turn and stare or freeze, gradually escalating his behavior to try to calm the puppy down. If the puppy doesn't recognize and adapt to these communications, there can easily be a fight between the two dogs.

## Walking in a Curve

We often force our dogs to walk straight toward each other on sidewalks or in other circumstances. For the dog, this is a very rude and confrontational behavior. This could be one reason so many owners have barking and lunging dogs when they are out for walks. It will help your dog if you allow him to walk in even a small curve, whether it is on the sidewalk, going across the street, or going into the grass or a driveway. The more anxious or concerned your dog, the bigger the curve should be.

## DID YOU KNOW?

Humans can use slow-moving behavior with fearful or shy dogs. In combination with several other behaviors, it can help a shy or anxious dog calm down and be more interactive. Other behaviors to use with especially shy or undersocialized dogs are turning away, yawning, avoiding direct eye contact, and getting down to their level so you are not leaning over them.

## Smiling

Smiling occurs when the front of a dog's face contracts up and down to show the teeth. The dog may also draw his lips back to show all of his teeth. The difference between this behavior and a dog that shows his teeth in a snarl is the rest of his body language. A snarling dog is stiff or crouched, with eyes dilated and looking scary overall. A smiling dog's body is relaxed and lowered with a low tail wag. His eyes will be soft and squinting slightly.

↑ 1. Fourteen-year-old Sadie sits to calm the rowdy puppy Bella.

↑ 2. Bella is ready to pounce. Sadie turns her back.

↑ 3. Bella's rowdy behavior escalates. Sadie tells Bella to "cut it out."

↑ 4. All's well.

## Urinating Submissively

At the ARL, we often get calls about submissive urination from frustrated owners who believe this is a house-training problem. It is very different, though, because the dog or puppy that rolls on his back or squats and urinates is being very respectful and as subordinate as he knows how to be. If a dog does this behavior to another dog, the other dog is satisfied and walks away. If we can learn to predict the behavior and change our approach to the dog, we can often teach a dog that he does not need to be this submissive with us.

↑ **Dogs do smile.**

When you come home and greet your dog, avoid eye contact and approach him from the side instead of the front. Squat or kneel down so you look less intimidating or threatening to him. Refrain from scolding him for urinating, because this will only make matters worse.

## Flirting

*Flirting* means that a dog is acting silly and puppy-like by jumping in the air, grabbing a toy to shake or toss, running in circles, and generally acting in a way that amuses us. Whether he's trying to get a person to laugh or another dog to play, his goal is to diffuse all confrontations and conflicts.

# Observing Your Dog

Dogs want us to understand them, and they may exaggerate their behaviors in an effort to help us. They will exaggerate their behaviors with other dogs, especially puppies, to give the other dogs a chance to understand them.

Dogs with little social interest in, experience with, or attraction to humans make no effort to make their behavior known. Dogs like this often have been considered

↑ Some dogs like belly rubs, while others may not want to expose their stomachs.

dangerous dogs who growl, attack, or bite "for no reason at all" because their signals are too subtle for humans to notice or understand. These dogs often end up in shelters, labeled "aggressive" by their owners.

Observe your dog's signals at home when you need to move him out of your way or when he has his toys, bones, or food bowl. If you scold your dog for some infraction, how does he react? That look is not guilt. He's not admitting to being "bad"; rather, it's an appeasement behavior with the intention of calming you down. Observing your dog's calming signals can be helpful on walks, at the veterinarian's clinic, and any time your dog meets new people, dogs, or other pets.

## Dogs Interacting with Dogs

Watching puppies playing is a great way to start observing signals. Whether it is a litter of siblings or a play group from a class, you may notice that all of them stop for a few seconds about every fifteen to twenty seconds. This isn't really a "freeze," but just stillness, and then they will start playing again. Watching these puppies allows you to see many behaviors, including sniffing, freezing, lip and nose licking, and play bowing.

↑  When a new dog comes into an area, if dogs are allowed to do their normal greeting
   and sniffing behaviors, usually everyone gets along fine.

Adult dogs will often stop playing for a few seconds, too, especially if a new dog comes into the group. Watch dogs at a dog park, especially if there is a group and a new dog approaches to play. The group will surround the new dog, sniffing him for a bit, and then everyone will take a break for a few seconds. Suddenly, one dog will do a play bow, and then everyone is off and running. Most dogs do not want a confrontation, and if allowed to do their normal greeting behaviors, they will get along just fine.

## Dogs on Leash

There can be trouble when dogs meet on leash. An owner concerned about how his or her dog will behave may crank the leash tightly and bring the dog in close. This will change the body language and communication between the two dogs. Pulling on the leash makes the dog strain against the collar, giving him the appearance of being aroused, intense, and possibly unfriendly. Allowing a loose leash gives a dog the freedom to display appropriate body language and prevent problems. Allowing the dogs to approach in a curve and sniff the ground, keeping things calm, will make the meeting smoother and friendlier.

↑ **Allow enough slack in the leash to let the dogs display normal greeting behavior.**

Also, while we want our dogs to be social and polite in public, they do not need to meet and interact with every dog along the way. Walking nicely beside you and ignoring the other dog is fine.

## Dogs Interacting with Children

Children are vulnerable because they approach dogs as if they are other children. A child usually wants to hug the dog, look in his eyes and ears, pick up his paws, and catch his tail. In canine language, this child is a young animal with very poor manners, and many dogs try to show their displeasure in very simple ways. Often, the first signal of concern is a dog freezing when a child tries to hug him. Everyone thinks the dog loves the interaction because he doesn't move away. The adults may assume that the child can hug the dog any time and will not notice any behavioral signs from the dog until he actually growls, lifts his lip in a snarl, or snaps at the child.

Watch for signals such as head turning, lip and nose licking, yawning, and freezing. Help the dog out if he is showing concern. Hand the child a toy or start a game with the dog. By doing this, you have changed the dog's concern and hopefully relieved his anxiety. You may also ask the child to leave the dog and do something else.

Ideally, here is what you might see when a child and dog meet and the dog is enjoying the interaction:

- When the child approaches the dog, the dog's whole body is included in the wagging tail. You see a dog whose whole body has become a wiggle.
- The dog's eyes are squinty, slightly closed, and blinking; his ears are soft and floppy or laid softly against his neck; and his tail is level with or below the height of his body and wagging smoothly from side to side or possibly in a circle.
- He is flexible, not frozen, and should approach the child as the child approaches him, unless restrained by his owner. Many dogs are close to eye level with toddlers and do not attempt to jump on the children because they can greet them face to face. A dog may check the child's hands for food, shoes to see where the child has been, and face and mouth to see what the child has been eating.
- If the child is familiar to the dog, and they usually play or cuddle, the dog may lie down to show his belly for a tummy scratch. We have seen dogs learn to control

↑    Adults need to supervise the interactions of young children with dogs.

# DOG TAILS

## Fox

I adopted Fox, my Chow Chow, from the ARL when she was about four months old. She had been brought into the shelter at about nine weeks old by a nice lady who had bought her from a breeder. The breeder had assured the woman that Chows were great with kids, and they look like little teddy bears, so after she brought Fox home, she let her kids take the puppy outside to play. I have no idea how much socialization Fox had had before going to her new home, but she was very frightened and learned quickly that if she struggled, growled, and snapped, the kids would leave her alone. The lady called the breeder, explaining how aggressive the puppy was toward her children.

She could return the puppy but couldn't get a refund, and she really felt that the man would just sell the puppy again and put another family through the grief of having to give up a puppy that was terrified of kids. So the woman turned the puppy over to the ARL, hoping that someone with no children could adopt her and she would be OK.

Fox eventually learned not to be so afraid of children, even though parents would occasionally recognize her breed and quickly lead their children away. Fox decided that, when she met children, she would lie down slowly and let them scratch her tummy, which kept the children from being in her face, and everyone had a good time.

When Fox met children in public spots, where I couldn't let her decide to roll on her back, I gently held her head and guided the children to her furry back and even her tail. She just really didn't want children staring into her big brown eyes or examining her dark blue tongue. (Chow Chows have blue-shaded tongues.)

## For More Info...

Refer to *On Talking Terms with Dogs: Calming Signals* by Turid Rugaas to explore more about recognizing your dog's communication signals.

↑　**A shelter volunteer supervises this meeting between a dog and potential adopters.**

children by offering their bellies to rub rather than trying to scare them away or threaten them.

Look for the following warning signals when a child is approaching, indicating that your dog is uncomfortable, nervous, or scared.

- The dog hurries to hide behind you.
- The dog shuts his mouth tightly.
- The dog's tail stops wagging, or he tucks it up under his belly.
- The dog's ears lay flat against the back of his head.
- The hair on the dog's back from his shoulders to his tail starts to stand up. Sometimes it is the whole length of his back; sometimes it is just on the shoulders and hips.
- The dog's eyes get big, he doesn't blink, and his pupils dilate, making each entire eye look black.
- The dog vocalizes, whether a whine or a bark.

Any or all of these signals show distress, fear, and alarm. Step in front of your

# WATCH HIS FACE

**Q:** My dog wags his tail and seems friendly to strange dogs when we are out walking, but when they get close to him, he growls, barks, and lunges. Why does he act friendly if he isn't?

**A:** When a dog is put in a situation in which he is uncomfortable, he has limited ways to communicate his concerns to us. Many dogs are not comfortable with face-to-face meetings with strange dogs and will give subtle but clear signs to their owners and the other dogs. When we ignore these signs, a dog must escalate his communication to make it perfectly clear that he doesn't want this meeting to happen.

Watch your dog's face and body language. Are his eyes wide open in alarm or slanted and squinty in friendliness? Is his mouth tight, lips tight to his teeth, lines showing below his eyes or on his forehead in concern? Or is he panting, mouth open, face and ears relaxed in greeting? Is he up on his toes, hair along his spine standing on end, stiffened in alarm? Or is he loose in his body, sitting or hanging out, relaxed and ready for play? The more we learn to read our canine's body language, the more he can rely on us to help him in different situations.

the child from approaching, and see if your dog can calm down. If the dog is still retreating, tell the child that your dog doesn't feel well and doesn't want to meet anyone right now, and walk your dog away. Going forward, you will want to work with your dog on helping him be happier and calmer around children.

If your dog sees a child approaching and he holds his tail up very high over his back, leans his body forward, holds his ears forward, and stands

← **A child's enthusiastic greeting may be too much for some dogs.**

↑　**With proper introductions and supervision, your adopted dog will fit right in with the family.**

that your dog is threatening to the child and that you should walk your dog away from the child. Some dogs just want to play but can be too rough for small children. Allow a child to approach only when the dog is in a Sit position and the child can pet his back or sides. The front paws of a large dog could scratch or injure a small child.

We always encourage owners to be a bit assertive with other people, especially regarding children approaching your dog. Even if your dog normally loves children, if you interpret his body language to indicate that he is concerned, help him out by asking the approaching child approaching to stand still for a moment. Then, using treats and your voice, praise your dog, steady his head, and allow the child to pet his sides or back in a gentle way. If more than one child approaches, have them take turns petting your dog, one at a time. Each situation can be different for your dog, and you may not see or understand if there are other stressful things going on around him.

# 3 Developmental Stages and Socialization

**M**ost of the information on raising, socializing, and training dogs starts after puppies are eight weeks or older—the age at which puppies are available to go to new homes. Much of a dog's personality, temperament, and abilities develop during those first eight weeks. Genetics and the mother dog have a large effect on the kind of pet your puppy will become. It's optimal if you can meet your puppy's mother during those early weeks and learn about her social, physical, and mental health. The best time to meet the mom and pick a puppy from the litter is when the pups are four to six weeks old; before then, the mother may be very protective of her pups and wary of strangers.

While all of this should be easy to do if you are purchasing a puppy from a breeder, it may not be possible when adopting from a shelter unless the mother dog came into the shelter when pregnant and gave birth either in the shelter or in a foster home. If this is the case, you will want to ask about the mother to find out as much as you can about her behavior, health, and temperament in the foster home.

The following sections are general guidelines to help you understand the stages in a puppy's development, early socialization, and training.

↑  **A pregnant female at day fifty-eight of gestation.**

# Gestation

Gestation lasts approximately sixty-two days. During this time, the mother should be well cared for in a safe, warm, comfortable whelping pen so she whelps her puppies without incident. She should be eating quality, high-protein food and visiting the veterinarian regularly.

# Birth to Twelve Days

Puppies are blind and deaf from birth to approximately twelve days old. Their sense of smell is good enough to find mom and nourishment and to start to learn about their environment through scent and touch. They need to be briefly handled each day and checked to be sure they are gaining weight. At around twelve days old, puppies begin to see and hear.

# Thirteen to Twenty Days

From thirteen to approximately twenty days, the puppies mostly eat, sleep, grow fast, and explore their environment. At this age, they should start to spend more time with

↑ **Pups are blind and deaf from birth but are able to smell right away.**

people and be handled individually. A few minutes of handling each day will make a huge difference in each puppy's future comfort level with humans. Feet, noses, and ears should be gently touched. Puppies begin to recognize people's voices and scents. They will begin to play with each other, and each puppy will start to show individual personalities and preferences. During this time, puppies should be protected from extreme cold and heat and very loud noises.

## Three Weeks to Seven Weeks

From twenty-one to forty-nine days, puppies change fast. They will gain coordination, and their senses are developing rapidly. They should be introduced to handling by many people, especially supervised children; meet gentle adult dogs; and get lots of individual attention. Any puppies that show fear or anxiety should get some extra handling and attention to help prevent behavior problems later in their lives.

The puppies' weights need to be monitored to be sure that all of the puppies are getting their share of nursing and food. At three to four weeks, the puppies are offered ground and soaked dog food (gruel). Each time they are offered food, they are

↑ **Boxer puppies at six weeks old.**

separated from their mom for a few minutes. The puppies may sniff and lick the food, but depending on their supply of mother's milk, they may not be interested in eating for the first few days. Usually by four weeks, they are eager to supplement milk with gruel and dig in.

Puppies can start learning to potty on grass by following Mom. They will sniff around, looking for the "right" spot, and should be praised gently for success. Before this age, their mother has been cleaning up the puppies' messes. She has already taught them to stay clean. Their instinct is to continue being clean, so the breeder or foster parent can introduce a crate containing soft old towels to the nest and play area. The puppies learn to go in and out of the crate, to sleep in it, and to potty away from that area.

At four to five weeks, each puppy is taken away from the litter for a few minutes so they can start to learn to be away from mom and littermates. The puppy is returned to the litter before he gets too upset. This helps the puppies get used to handling by humans and prepares them for weaning.

At this age, humans can gently start some basic training with the puppies. For example, if a puppy cries or barks, the person should wait until the puppy is quiet before responding. In this way, the puppies are already learning that barking, whining, or crying sends humans away, and quiet brings them closer.

Another example is that the person waits until a puppy is sitting before petting him or picking him up. This teaches that puppy that sitting gets attention and jumping up does not. This is very hard with puppies. Who doesn't want to pick up a puppy that puts his little front paws on your foot or leg for attention?

Ideally, the puppies' caretaker will take them to the veterinarian for a social visit and their first vaccinations and worming. They may even go for a second social visit for the staff to play with and handle them so the puppies do not fear their visits to the veterinarian.

Staying with their mother for at least seven weeks is vital for best results in a puppy's life. During that last week, a puppy starts to learn that nipping mom and his littermates with those sharp teeth hurts if he uses too much pressure. His littermates walk away, isolating the biting puppy. He learns to soften his bite (called *bite inhibition*) so the others will continue to play with him.

During that last week, he also learns that mom is not the big softy he thought she was. She can and will growl, snarl, snap, and even bite him if his behavior is too rough or otherwise inappropriate. From this experience with her, he should begin

## Supervision Mandatory

When puppies of this age meet children, parents should be especially aware of their interactions and always be there to supervise. Small children could accidentally hurt a puppy, even in play. Parents must also watch for signs of stress and fear in the pups and move them to a quiet place as they explain appropriate handling and play to the children. Even friendly, social pups can nip or bite if cornered and frightened or handled roughly. Positive, fun-for-all experiences should be the goal here. Puppies should not be expected to entertain children for more than a few minutes at a time, with frequent breaks for potty, water, and snacks.

to learn to be appropriate with other adult dogs, although it is likely the puppy will need several experiences with adult dogs to learn not to jump, bite, or chew on them.

## Seven to Ten Weeks

At eight weeks, puppies can start going to their new homes, although many experts advise keeping small-breed puppies longer, partly because they are just so tiny.

Once in their new homes, puppies learn quickly. They need to meet many people to help them learn to enjoy being around people. A new puppy adopter should start simple, positive training, ideally in a well-run class with a few other puppies of similar age for socialization. When you attend a puppy class, you will probably be doing as much listening as training. The instructors will try to answer any questions that you or other participants have. Trading successes, tips, and frustrations can be very beneficial for you as well as your puppy.

↑   **Shelter puppies should be curious about visitors.**

You can teach and reinforce the basics, like Sit and Down, to your puppy very quickly at this age. Puppies are very willing learners and eager to be with their humans. Remember that your puppy has a pretty short attention span, so be patient and train in frequent short sessions at home.

Overlapping this stage is another stage that runs from about eight weeks through eleven weeks. It is commonly called a *fear imprint period*. If your puppy reacts to an experience with fear or anxiety, you need to respond and help the puppy become less fearful. For example, if a child accidentally steps on the puppy, the puppy might react with fear, even to the point of growling or bolting. If possible (and if the puppy is not seriously hurt), you should bring the puppy back to the child and, using gentle voices, treats, and toys, reintroduce the puppy to the child in a very positive way. Anything that happens to the puppy, whether traumatic or positive, can have a lasting effect. Every effort to make life experiences fun is a great investment in the puppy's future.

## Troubleshooting

If you are concerned that your puppy's behavior seems excessive, or he is growling or biting, you may want to call an experienced trainer or behavior expert for help.

## Ten to Sixteen Weeks

From ten to sixteen weeks, puppies are starting to get new teeth. They use their mouths and teeth extensively to explore their environment and to help ease the discomfort of the new teeth erupting. Your puppy may bite you or other pets to try to get his way. The puppy learned bite inhibition from his mother and littermates, but you'll still need to provide a lot of structure, gentle but consistent leadership, and supervision to get through the teething stage. (See Nothing in Life Is Free in Chapter 8.) Continued socialization with other puppies and adult dogs keeps reinforcing what is and what is not acceptable.

At this stage, your puppy is starting to be brave about leaving you. If you think that your puppy has been successfully trained not to leave your side, think again! You will find that your puppy is willing to wander off, leaving you for more exciting scents, sights, and sounds. Many puppies become lost at this age (hopefully just temporarily), because they are testing the boundaries. You want to make sure that your puppy is safely confined when outside, but *never* leave a puppy tied up outdoors.

↑  Monitor what a twelve-week-old puppy puts in his mouth, because not everything he chooses will be safe.

There is a time in a puppy's life where he seems to have "puppy license" to get away with some naughty behaviors with other dogs. Many adult dogs, especially males, it seems, will tolerate puppy biting, jumping, climbing, tail pulling, and other obnoxious behaviors that the dog would not allow from another adult dog. Usually, at about five to seven months, this puppy license "expires." Adult dogs start to treat the puppy like a juvenile delinquent and will stop rude puppy behaviors.

When an adult dog stops allowing these behaviors, many owners misinterpret what the adult dog is doing. The adult may look like he is going to hurt the puppy, and the puppy often squeals, falls on his back, and acts like he is being hurt. As scary as this scenario is, your puppy needs to know his boundaries with adult dogs. These are lessons that he will remember. Scolding or punishing an adult dog that is just doing his job by training the puppy is a mistake. It can turn your puppy into a bully.

## Sixteen Weeks to Eight Months

At some time between sixteen weeks and eight months, most puppies go through a *flight instinct period*, also commonly called a *testing period*. This is the time when a

# The Importance of Training

Dogs that have not had the benefit of training and socialization before adulthood are the ones that often get turned into shelters. We get calls from owners who are having problems with dogs that have suddenly become territorial or protective or have started guarding their toys, food bowls, beds, and even their humans from other dogs and people. They are described in ways such as "not trainable," "hyper," "vicious," "suddenly aggressive," and various other terms that usually indicate poor socialization and lack of training. These dogs have stayed in their homes because they were cute and cuddly as puppies, but, as adults without guidance, structure, and training, they appear dangerous to their owners.

puppy seems to have forgotten house-training, manners, and anything else previously taught. He might bite, run, ignore your cues, and resist any efforts to rein him in. This is an adolescent stage that can negatively affect your bond with your puppy if you don't remember that it is *only temporary*.

Your sweet puppy will come back. The stage usually lasts only one or two weeks, even though it seems permanent. Many physical changes occur; your puppy is

↑   Your resident adult dog will likely tolerate a newly adopted youngster's "puppy behavior" while he is still small.

Once a dog enters a shelter and shows aggressive behaviors, he becomes a concern. How easily this could have been avoided with early training and socialization!

growing so fast during this time. Remember, he is still teething, with the big molars coming in. He may be having pain and discomfort. He may destroy new toys in minutes, so you'll need to give him tougher toys.

He is still a puppy. He needs structure, love, and training. Don't forget exercise, as his needs for games and stimulation will grow during this time. Maintain but carefully supervise playtime with other compatible puppies and dogs. Give your puppy one- or two-minute time-outs if he gets too rough.

Overlapping this stage is a second fear stage that often occurs between six months and fourteen months. Sometimes puppies that have never shown fear of strangers, dogs, or places will exhibit fear now. Even with familiar people, the puppy may suddenly be unfriendly, growl, and show fear. Continue classes. Keep

↑ Be ready to redirect your six-month-old puppy to appropriate behavior as needed.

# When to Spay or Neuter?

Shelters spay or neuter young dogs around eight weeks of age and always before adoption. A female will go into *estrus*, or *heat*, anywhere from six months to a year old. If she hasn't been spayed, she can get pregnant during this time, even if it's her first heat. Male dogs will be very creative trying to reach a female in heat, even climbing fences or digging into kennels to get to her. Male puppies that have not been neutered may start to lift their legs to mark vertical objects, especially if they see other male dogs.

training with a gentle voice, treats, and toys and be positive, but avoid forcing the issue if the puppy shows fear.

If he is fearful, wait a couple of weeks to introduce him to new people but continue practicing what you've taught him in situations where he is fearful. If you act very "matter of fact" and expect him to act the same way, it can help get him through this stage. Just don't punish him when he is afraid or act disappointed if he can't perform now as he did before. Reward any effort on his part. Help him be successful, even if you are stepping back in your training to an earlier phase. Praise and reward his efforts during this period.

## Adulthood: Twelve Months and Older

A puppy is considered an adult starting at one year of age, even though many dogs don't mentally or emotionally mature until two years of age or even older. Some breeds have individuals that never seem to act like adults; for example, Golden Retrievers are perpetual puppies and are cherished for it.

# 4 Choosing Your New Dog

You will find dogs of all breeds, ages, sizes, colors, characteristics, abilities, and temperaments at an animal shelter. These dogs come from a variety of sources. Some of them are picked up as strays, some of them come from people who need to rehome their pets for various reasons, some of them come from people whose dogs have had accidental litters of puppies.

According to recent statistics reported on the ASPCA's website (*www.aspca. org*), about 3.3 million dogs enter shelters every year, and about half this number are adopted each year. While that is not bad, the shelter world wants to see that number increased because there are still millions of dogs that never find homes and are euthanized. Just the right dog or puppy may be in a shelter waiting for you.

When you enter a shelter, you should have some idea of what type of dog you are looking for. If you don't have a basic plan for the kind of dog that will fit best in your home, you could make an impulsive choice that you will regret. Looking at those sad and needy eyes in the kennels can be a challenge, and walking away from them is heart-wrenching. If you do have room for a dog in your home, here are some ideas to help you make an informed decision to ensure that your new pet becomes a permanent part of your family. Keep in mind that choosing the right puppy is quite different from choosing the right adolescent or adult dog.

↑  With so many adorable shelter dogs, you can't choose based on looks alone.

## Choosing a Puppy
### Genetics

Knowing your puppy's genetic background may be important if you have a specific activity in mind for him. However, every dog is an individual, so personality and instinct will vary from dog to dog even within the same breed. In the end, how a dog behaves is a combination of nature and nurture, so it's important to look at the puppy in front of you instead of creating expectations from its breed or appearance.

→  If you did not know that this was a Rottweiler/Pit Bull puppy, you might have a hard time guessing his lineage.

# Breed Behaviors

While there is something to be said for both nature and nurture on how any particular puppy turns out, nature does rule in some areas, especially when purebred puppies are concerned. For example, an English Springer Spaniel puppy and a Border Collie puppy will react very differently toward a sheep. The spaniel may lick the sheep or try to get it to play with a toy, but the Border Collie will instinctively attempt some form of herding behavior.

How much can you learn about a shelter puppy's genetics? Sometimes, nothing at all. Sometimes the shelter staff knows the parents of puppies available for adoption, or they may at least know the puppies' mother. A single litter of puppies can have more than one father, so even in one litter, there can be a big variation in breed, size, and personality. Another interesting factor is when both parents are mixed breeds, and the puppies do not look anything like either one of them.

## Personality

You have made a decision about the type of dog you want, and the shelter has a litter of puppies that might fit your criteria. So, out of eight puppies in the litter,

↑   Visit a shy puppy away from his littermates, so you can see his personality.

## Adoption Tip

To avoid making a hasty decision, leave the children at home when you make your first visit to the shelter. Screen the puppy or dog and know that he is a good fit for your family before the kids meet him.

how do you decide which one is best for you? As we've mentioned, personalities of puppies in the same litter can be dramatically different.

Most shelters do not allow visitors to enter puppy pens, but you can observe the litter. Look for a puppy that is trying to make eye contact, being social, and working for attention while getting closer to you. If possible, pick up a puppy, hold him so that you can look into his eyes, and evaluate his response.

If some of the puppies are shy when they are in the group, don't automatically rule them out. Visiting with them separately can give them a chance to show their personalities without the competition of their littermates. Conversely, puppies that seem outgoing or demanding while in the pen can turn out to be quite shy and

↑    A potential adopter and puppy get to know each other better in the
      ARL's "hug room."

nervous when meeting with you outside the pen. Puppies need to be brought out of their comfort zone to see how they adjust to new people and environments.

A puppy might try to lick your face, or he might freeze and seem to go stiff, get frantic and panicky, or even urinate out of fear. If he does show fear, does he recover in a few seconds and maybe start licking you, wagging his tail, and interacting with you? If he shows fear and nothing you do seems to help, we recommend meeting another puppy.

If you want to put extra effort into caring for, training, and socializing a puppy who may never act like a "normal" dog, the shyest pup may be your dog. If you want a running buddy who's ready to play at the drop of a hat, the boldest pup of the litter might be for you.

## Adoption Tip

The bottom line is that choosing a puppy is a bit of a guessing game. If you have firm expectations about what you want or need in a canine companion, such as size restrictions, you should consider an adult dog.

# The Right Dog for You

Whether you plan to adopt a puppy, a young adult, or an older dog, you must first consider the following:

- Where do you live? A city apartment? A surburban home? In the country? Your home and lifestyle are important considerations.

- What size dog are you comfortable with?

- What size dog best fits your home and outdoor space?

- What activity level do you want? Do you have the time to exercise an energetic small dog? An energetic large dog? Sometimes smaller dogs are more active than larger ones.

- How much time to you have to devote to coat care? Will you take a dog to be professionally groomed? Do you mind if a dog sheds? If you don't have a few minutes, several days a week, to at least brush your dog, you should look for a dog that requires minimal coat care. A quick bath once in a while and a quick comb-through to collect the shedding hair a couple times a week are all that some dogs need, while others may need regular professional grooming. If the latter, you must consider the cost and frequency of professional grooming before adopting the dog. We often see dogs surrendered because their owners underestimated their grooming needs, and the dogs may be badly matted, have skin injuries or ear infections, or have other issues.

- What about noise? Do you want a dog that is quiet or one that barks?

- Do you want a male or a female? There are many opinions, and, as with most of the other choices, it comes down to personal preference.

In general, though, the average family should look for a puppy that is cuddly, outgoing, and interested in being near you but not obnoxious. The way a pup interacts helps create the bond that lasts a lifetime.

Keep in mind that the evaluations done with puppies in a shelter do not guarantee what their personalities will be like when they are grown. No one has been able to devise an evaluation for puppies that consistently predicts their adult personalities and talents. Remember, genetics play a part, as does socialization before and after weaning and separation from the mother and littermates.

## Adopting an Adult Dog

Adopting an adult dog has many advantages. You will be able to spend some time with the dog, and you will know for certain how big he is. You will be able to see if

↑  **Adopting a wonderful older dog can be the best decision for a family.**

## Jerry

Jerry came to the ARL to find a new dog after his longtime animal companion died. The dog shown here, Romeo, had been surrendered to the ARL. This photo was taken of them just after they met in one of the ARL's "hug rooms." In just a few short minutes, Jerry and Romeo formed one of those instant bonds that every dog lover understands. You can see it in their smiles.

he is friendly, has fears that need to be worked on, needs obedience training, or will need hours of exercise each day. In general, you will be able to tell who this dog is.

While adopting an adult dog means missing out on that cute "baby" stage, it enables you to make a rational, less emotional decision, and it can be just as much a "love at first sight" experience as with a puppy.

Adult dogs are usually at the shelter because a caring owner had no other choice. Most of the dogs in the shelter were good house dogs, are house-trained, have been around people, and simply need a home. If they weren't, they probably would have lost their homes long before age three. They likely would be great additions to adoptive families.

Sometimes these dogs are overlooked because people hesitate to fall in love with a dog they might not have for as many years as they would a puppy. They miss the opportunity to enjoy these dogs and enrich their own lives.

## Selecting a Purebred Pooch

Did you know that, nationwide, about 30 percent of dogs and puppies in shelters are purebred dogs? So if you want to adopt a purebred, shelters are a great place to look. We have had many purebred puppies surrendered to the ARL.

If local shelters don't have the breed you want, check breed-specific rescue groups in your area. Many of these groups promote their available dogs on websites like *Petfinder. com* and *Petango.com* as well as on their own websites. Research the advice given on breed rescue websites. The rescue groups often will spell out the reality of living with the breed because they want people to know the facts before taking one of their dogs home.

# 5 Getting Ready for Your Adopted Dog

## Supplies You'll Need

You've picked out your new family member and are ready to start incorporating him into your household. To help make this transition as smooth as possible, we recommend that you have some supplies on hand before you bring the dog home.

### Bowls

Buy a sturdy bowl that doesn't tip easily; high-quality stainless steel is a good choice for both food and water bowls because it is durable and easy to clean. Some people prefer heavy ceramic bowls because they won't

tip over and a dog can't pick them up and carry them around, but the coatings on some ceramic bowls can contain lead, a harmful metal. Plastic bowls are not recommended. Whatever type of bowls you choose, make sure that they are made of quality, nontoxic materials.

## Food

Look for a dog food that is labeled "complete" and read the ingredients list. It is important to remember that the first three ingredients listed on the package make up the majority of the food. The ARL, as well as many shelters, will let you know what food your dog has been eating while at the shelter. If he has been doing well on this food, you may want to continue it at home. If you choose to change your dog's food, do your research and ask your veterinarian for advice; the varieties of dog food are endless. Make any dietary changes gradually, increasing the ratio of new food to old food over a period of time, to avoid causing your dog digestive upset.

# DOG TAILS

## Microchip Miracle

One summer, a man found a tiny Pekingese huddled in the middle of a residential street in a town in Iowa near our shelter. He brought her to our staff, sure that there was an owner looking for her. Little did he know that she had been lost from her home in Las Vegas, Nevada, for more than a year. Her name was Toy, and she was about fourteen years old. The microchip that stored her owner's information gave us the opportunity to call him. He dropped everything to fly to Des Moines to get her. It was a miracle for Toy and her family, but certainly a mystery that will never be solved. Just how did Toy leave her Las Vegas home and end up in Des Moines? Without a microchip, there would have been no hope of getting her back to the people who loved her.

## Collar, Leash, and Identification

When your pet is ready to leave the shelter, be sure to have a collar, leash, and tags with your pet's name and your contact information. Some shelters will microchip dogs before they leave for their new homes. A microchip is a permanent form of ID that is implanted under the dog's skin between the shoulder blades. Animal shelters, veterinary clinics, and animal-control offices are equipped with scanners that will detect the number on a lost dog's chip. Calling the microchip registry with that code should get the lost pet back to his owner quickly.

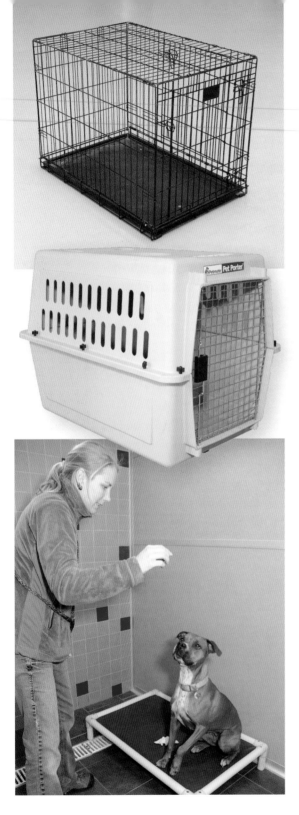

Your dog should never be without his identification. Some owners remove their dogs' collars when they are indoors, but if a dog escapes the house and has no collar or ID tag, a person who finds him will not have the owner's contact information. However, a microchip gives your dog a second chance that he will be returned safely to you.

## Crate

Be sure to select the right size crate for your dog. There are two main types of crates used for house-training and confinement: metal-wire folding crates or solid plastic crates with windows and metal-wire doors. Plastic crates are the type used for dogs traveling or being shipped by air.

A third type of crate, soft fabric, can be used with dogs that are accustomed to being crated and won't try to chew or dig their way out. Fabric crates are easily damaged from the inside, so they are never a good choice for young puppies or for dogs

↑ A metal crate has a solid bottom and folds up for easy transport.

↖ A plastic crate has a wire door and "windows" along the sides and back.

← Sturdy, easy-to-clean, elevated beds (such as Kuranda™ beds) are often used in shelters.

that may be anxious to get out. Refer to Crate Training in Chapter 8 to help get your dog settled, happy, and comfortable in a crate.

## Bed

A rug or mat is a fine first bed for your puppy; make sure it is something that you can clean easily. Raised beds, like the one pictured on page 64, are easy to clean and fairly indestructible. Many shelters use this type of bed. If using this type of bed at home, you could add bedding to make it more comfortable or attractive to your dog. Other beds resemble large pillows and come in a variety of sizes to fit all kinds of dogs. Pet-supply stores carry a variety of beds to choose from.

## Toys

There are many toys available that are safe and useful for keeping pets busy. Tough rubber toys are very popular, and they come in many sizes and shapes. These toys are durable, but not indestructible, so supervise your dog's chewing as well as the condition of the toy. If your dog is breaking off small pieces that he could swallow, it's time to replace the toy.

↑ **Supervise your dog when he is playing with soft or stuffed toys, or this could be the result.**

↑ **Pull toys teach the puppy to chase and catch the toy—and not the child.**

Some dog toys dispense treats or kibble if tipped or rolled around, so they give your dog some mental stimulation as he learns what to do to get the food out. These toys are a safe way to entertain a dog of any age. You could even feed your dog one of his meals in a food-dispensing toy. To occupy your dog for a longer period of time, fill the toy with peanut butter and freeze it before giving it to him.

Rawhides have been used for a long time as chew toys, but concerns about the toxic chemicals used to process hides have professionals and owners looking for alternatives. Ask your pet-supply store about chews that are appropriate and safe for your dog or puppy. Get chews that are oversized for your pet and discard them as they get smaller. A dog may be tempted to swallow part of a chew toy if he thinks it is small enough. Trying to grab a wet, slippery chew toy as it is being swallowed can be dangerous and difficult.

Puzzle toys are also available for dogs. With a puzzle toy, you can hide treats in small compartments, and your dog has to find them and figure out how to get them out. The key is to find puzzle toys that engage your dog's mind and entertain, rather than frustrate, him.

Put out a few toys at a time and rotate them. Keep them in a drawer and switch them every other day to keep them "new" for your dog.

## First-Aid Kit

Do you know what to do if your pet is choking or if he ate something that might be poisonous? If not, check with your local American Red Cross to find out if they offer pet first-aid classes. Keep the following important phone numbers and supplies in your pet first-aid kit in a handy spot:

- The toll-free number for the Animal Poison Control Center: 888-426-4435
- Your veterinarian's number and a number for a local emergency or after-hours clinic
- A copy of your pet's most recent medical records
- Several rolls of gauze, adhesive tape for bandages, nonstick bandages, and towels or strips of clean cloth
- A bottle of milk of magnesia and hydrogen peroxide (*Note:* Do not use these products unless directed by a veterinarian. Using the wrong product could cause more harm than good.)
- A digital rectal pet thermometer
- An eye dropper or oral syringe for administering medications or fluids, as directed by your veterinarian
- A muzzle that fits your dog or an old necktie, soft strips of cloth, or a nylon stocking for making a muzzle
- An extra leash (or several, if you have more than one dog)

# DID YOU KNOW?

If you need to use first aid on your pet, always follow up by contacting your veterinarian for more information or an examination. First aid is not meant to replace veterinary care, but it can save your pet's life, giving you time to get help from a veterinarian.

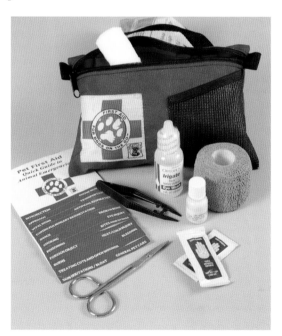

# DID YOU KNOW?

If your dog is injured, he may bite out of fear or pain. The muzzle will keep you safe. We recommend using treats and conditioning to get your dog used to the feel of a muzzle. Then, in an emergency, he is less likely to be even more stressed by the muzzle.

## On Your Way Home

The moment you put your new dog in the car to go home, he is learning. We recommend that you confine your dog in the car from the beginning so he learns that it's not OK to roam free about the car. It is dangerous for your dog to climb onto your lap, lie under your feet, or hang out the window while you are driving. A dog roaming freely in the car is vulnerable in an emergency. If you hit the brakes or get in a crash, the dog becomes a flying object that can be killed going through the windshield or can injure you or your passengers. A dog can also be injured or killed on the roadway if he gets out of the vehicle.

Owners who allow their dog to hang his head out the window are putting the dog at risk. Bugs can get in the dog's face, eyes, or ears, or, if he is

↑　Be sure that your dog is confined safely in the car. We recommend using a crate.

# Moving to a New Home

Pets can certainly experience the stress related to moving. Follow the tips below to make the move easier on all members of the family.

- Keep your dog on his regular schedule before the move and return to this schedule as soon as possible after moving. The familiarity and routine will reduce his stress level.

- On the day of the move, confine your dog to a familiar room where he feels safe. This will keep him out from underfoot as well as help him remain calm.

- If possible, your dog should be in a crate during the move. Put some of his favorite toys and blankets—something that smells familiar—in the crate.

- If you are planning to stay in any hotels, make sure that they accept pets ahead of time. Do not leave your dog in the car overnight for any reason.

- When you arrive at your new home, place your dog's food bowl, bed, and other items in a similar location to that of the previous home.

- Walk your dog around the house, yard, and neighborhood to orient him to his new home.

- Keep an eye on your dog. Be prepared to deal with any potty accidents without scolding. Sticking to your dog's schedule as closely as possible should keep accidents to a minimum.

leaning far enough out the window, he could be injured by other vehicles or things outside the car.

## His First Time at Home

When you first arrive home with your new pet, be sure he is on a leash before you open the car door. Many newly adopted dogs have escaped when owners open the car door without realizing that the dog may bolt. If the dog is confined in a crate or is on a leash, you can release him from the car with guidance, and he will start to learn that this is the procedure. You must control and carefully supervise his exit from the car.

↑ **Lead your dog to the potty spot you choose before you take him into the house.**

Before entering the house, lead the dog directly to the outdoor spot that you want him to use as his potty spot. If he is a puppy, carry him to the potty spot. After an exciting car ride, chances are your dog will need to urinate, and this is the perfect opportunity to set the pattern for him.

When you go inside, take a tour of the house with the dog on a leash. Let him sniff around the rooms and the furniture. If he is a male dog, he might lift his leg to mark a vertical surface. Clap your hands or make a big "uh-uh!" noise, which will startle him a bit, and you can then quickly walk him back to the potty spot outside. Plan to make a few trips outside this way during the first couple of hours, and it will help your dog understand the rules. Even a house-trained adult dog will need supervision and reminders in a new location. For a house-training a puppy, see Chapter 7.

Take treats with you when you take the dog outside. I recommend taking the dog out on a leash at first, even if you have a fenced yard. Guide the dog to the place you want him to go and give him a treat or a few minutes of play as a reward for doing his job. If he wants to go back inside, use that as a reward for doing his job quickly outdoors. If he wants to do more sniffing and play outdoors, use that as a reward for a

# Puppy-Proof Your Home

Make sure that your home is safe for your puppy. Check the location of electrical cords that he could chew and make them inaccessible to him. Make sure that he cannot get into garbage cans, cabinets, and drawers. Keep any household cleaning products and chemicals locked away where the puppy cannot get to them.

quick potty job. You will quickly learn what will be rewarding to your dog, and you can use those rewards to help train other behaviors.

Your new dog may be initially reluctant to potty on a short leash with you standing next to him. You might have to try a long 10- to 15-foot (3 to 4.5-m) line. Ignore the dog but watch him out of the corner of your eye as he wanders around to find the right spot. A quiet bit of praise when he does go will help him learn that you want him to relieve himself while you are nearby. This can be difficult for some dogs to work through. It is certainly stressful for a new owner to try to remedy when the dog won't potty outdoors for him or her.

↑ When it comes to chewing, an old shoe is the same as a new shoe to a dog. Put all shoes out of his reach and give him appropriate toys to chew on.

The first few days in a new home are stressful for any dog or puppy, as well as for the owners. In addition to the house-training protocol, watch to be sure your new pet is chewing on his toys and not on your shoes, telephone, remote control, couch, or anything else. Even if he picks up an old shoe that you don't care about, take it away and replace it with one of his own toys or a treat. Shoes are shoes, and old is the same as new to your dog; if you let him chew on an old shoe, he will think that all shoes are fair game. Old socks and slippers fall into the same category. Put away items in which he might be interested and keep two or three toys close by so you can help him learn what is OK to play with.

Plan your adoption for a time when you and other family members will be able to spend time with your new dog. Try not to bring the dog home one day and be gone for eight or nine hours the next. From the dog's point of view, you are abandoning him, and he may panic.

If possible, take a few days off of work and set up a schedule for house-training the dog as well as for leaving him alone for short periods of time. Put the dog where he is going to be, such as his crate or a gated-off room, when you are gone. Pick up your purse or keys or whatever items you take with you when you leave the house and go out the door. Count to fifty and then come back into the house. Speak quietly and calmly to the dog, no matter what he is doing. Clip a leash to him and

take him out to his potty spot. Every time you return, part of the routine should be to take him to that spot. He will start to learn that when you are gone longer and longer, you will still get him outdoors right away, so he will learn to wait for you to get home to relieve himself.

## Introducing Your New Dog to Resident Pets

A big consideration before adopting a new dog or puppy is how your current pets will receive the new addition to the family. You can make a big impact on how this transition goes. Here are some common scenarios:

- **Scenario one:** The family adopts a second dog, and the resident dog has been the only pet for several years.
- **Scenario two:** The family adopts a puppy. The resident cat(s) have never met a dog.
- **Scenario three:** The family adopts a puppy. The resident pets are an older dog and a cat that have gotten along fine for several years.

While these are only a few of the many possible adoption situations, our first priority in any scenario is safety for all pets and humans involved. Our second priority is to keep stress levels down for everyone. Here are some tips to help you get started:

1. All dogs, both resident and newly adopted, should be on a leash when you bring the new dog home. Ideally, you should have one handler for each dog before the new dog enters the home.

2. All dogs should have met on neutral territory or at the shelter before you completed the adoption, to ensure that all are compatible. However, compatibility can change, depending on location, the presence of toys or food, and the people present. Dogs want to keep their own "stuff" and not let a newcomer have it. That is pretty normal. Some growling and posturing is to be expected, but will any of the dogs start a fight? Keeping

↑ Ideally, the dogs will meet before the adoption is finalized. At a shelter compatibility test, both dogs are on leash at a safe distance apart for the introductions. The handlers wait for the dogs to establish eye contact before allowing them to come together to meet.

the dogs on leash can help get them out of a tense situation without risking someone having to put their hands into the mix.

3. All humans should do their best to remain calm, speak in low voices, and keep any excitement out of the situation.

4. Feed the dogs in separate bowls in separate parts of the room or the house. Even dogs that don't guard their food won't like another dog coming around to steal their portion. It is one of the easiest things you can do to prevent friction between dogs.

5. If you have cats, prepare a safe place for them to get away from the new puppy or dog. It is also a good idea to have the dog on a leash in case you need to prevent him from chasing the cat. This is for the safety of the cat, but it also gives you a chance to help the dog learn to leave the cat alone. Reward and reinforce that behavior.

6. Do not scold or punish any of the pets for their behavior. Control, modify, and desensitize them to help them learn to live comfortably with each other. If you have concerns, contact a behavior professional.

## DID YOU KNOW?

By nature, dogs are predators, and it will be normal for them to be aroused by the movements, smells, and sounds of small pets such as rabbits, hamsters, or guinea pigs. If you have any small pets, don't ever leave them alone with your new dog. Even the most gentle, laid-back dog can get into hunting mode if the opportunity is in front of him.

## Sleeping Arrangements

Where will your new pet sleep? Many dog owners choose to have their dogs sleep in crates, and that is often a good choice, especially because you aren't sure about your new dog's potty habits. Confinement is key in helping the dog learn to sleep through the night and wait until morning. Spend some time introducing your dog to a crate, using treats and praise (see Crate Training in Chapter 8).

Placement of the crate can make a huge difference for the puppy or dog. If you are bringing home a puppy that has just been taken from his mother and littermates, isolating him in a crate and putting the crate in a distant spot from your bedroom will make him miserable. Probably feeling abandoned and lonely, he may bark, howl, whine, whimper, and generally make noise all night. Just when he settles down, he

↑   **Have a safe place for your cat to rest while getting acquainted with a new pet.**

will hear a noise, and it will start all over again. If the crate is far enough away from your bedroom, you may not hear the commotion, but your pet is miserable.

A better option would be to set your dog's crate (or maybe a second crate) in the bedroom of an adult family member. Having a person present doesn't automatically

↑  **Set up your new dog's sleeping area near you for comfort, company, and quiet.**

make it OK for the puppy, but a few comforting words can really help. However, resist the temptation to take a whimpering, whining puppy out of the crate and into bed with you. Retraining a dog to sleep in a crate after a night or two in a big, cushy bed can be problematic. He will strongly resist being isolated back in the crate, even if you are right beside him in your bed.

Plan on a few nights of interrupted sleep until the puppy understands the routine. Most puppies can sleep through the night at approximately three months of age.

Before that, if he gets restless, sniffs, and makes a commotion, it might mean he needs to potty. Carry the puppy to the potty spot, set him down, and wait quietly until he goes. Carry him back and put him into the crate. This is not a time for treats or play. Remember that you are setting a pattern for the way you want to live with your dog. It is best to keep him in his crate during the night.

A similar setup can work for a new older puppy or adult dog. If he is isolated far from where his humans are sleeping, he may bark or howl for hours, looking for company. If he is sleeping in the same room with someone, he will usually be calmer

and quiet down more quickly. A benefit of getting an older puppy or adult dog is that he probably won't have to go out to relieve himself overnight.

## Outdoor Areas

A dog should never live his life on a chain. Chaining a dog outside 24/7 can lead to serious health and behavior problems for the dog. When it comes to health, the weight of the chain can strain the dog's neck and back. The rubbing of the collar against his neck can cause skin irritation, hair loss, and sores. A tangled chain can prevent the dog from getting to water and shelter, which can be potentially fatal during weather extremes. A dog that spends long amounts of time on a chain shows increased anxiousness and agitation, which can lead to more aggressive behavior. Such a dog also tends to have little to no human interaction, which leads to unsocial behavior and deprives him of the opportunity to build the bond that is essential to human-pet relationships.

If it is necessary to keep your dog outdoors for periods of time, keep these points in mind:

↑  A secure, shaded outdoor kennel provides a safe space outdoors for your dog.

- **Shelter**—Provide your dog with a secure outdoor kennel.
- **Placement**—Place the kennel in close proximity to the house, so the dog will be able to see and hear the family and vice versa.
- **Elements**—During hot days, make sure that your dog has shade, either from a tree, a commercial sun shade, or a covering for the top of the kennel. A kiddie pool filled with water will provide relief as well as entertainment. Always check to see that your dog has plenty of drinking water. In cold weather, a dog house with straw bedding will help keep your pet warm and dry.

# 6 Children and Dogs

Children and dogs can be amazing together. There is no question that they can be good for each other, but there are some key points to consider before bringing a dog into a family with children.

- Children do not understand dog language, and dogs do not understand children's language. Adults should always supervise their interactions.

- Teach the children how to pet your new dog. Children often go to pet a dog on the head, but it can be irritating to the dog. Instead, teach them to rub his shoulders, back, and sides, or his belly if he will roll over to show his tummy. Teach them not to handle the tail, feet, ears, mouth, or eyes.

- You must teach your children what a dog's behavior—even the most obvious things, like growling or snapping—means and how they should react. A child must know that when a dog is growling or showing his teeth, it may be a sign that he is ready to bite. The child should stop whatever he or she is doing, freeze, count to five, and then back away from the dog slowly and calmly. A child should never stare at or turn his or her back to the dog.

- Children under the age of seven should be supervised at all times with any dog, even the family dog.

- Dogs know that children run and are fun to chase. Children scream and squeal. They sometimes hit, pinch, or hold on to a dog's body parts, even if the dog struggles. Children like to hug dogs, kiss their noses, and even blow in their faces.

- Children and dogs both love to play tug-of-war, but it can escalate into a dangerous scene, even if done in play, because the dog will regrip his end of the tug and could bite the child's fingers.
- Children must never wrestle with the dog or try to get a toy away from him. Teach children to stay out of the dog's bed and crate, to stay away from his food bowls unless supervised, and especially to leave the dog alone if he is chewing on a bone or toy. A dog will protect the things that are important to him, even to the point of biting. It is helpful to teach your dog to "trade" (see Chapter 8) so that he learns to give up one thing to receive another. This is positive behavior to teach to both children and dogs.
- Don't do anything to your dog that you don't want your children to copy. If your dog isn't great about having his toenails trimmed, wait to trim them until the kids aren't around. You don't want the children to try to trim the dog's nails when you aren't watching (you also don't want the dog to associate the presence of the

↑  **A running child can incite a dog's desire to chase.**

children with a task he finds unpleasant). Some things that your dog will tolerate from an adult won't go as well with the kids.

- Sending the kids and dog outdoors to play in the yard happens in families everywhere, every day. But sometimes one of the children is bitten or scratched by the dog, and even if the dog is playing, it can mean that the owners will want to get rid of the dog. We expect so much from our dogs, and it is easy to forget that they are dogs, not babysitters, and they don't have a sense of what is right or wrong when it comes to children.

## Appropriate Games for Children and Dogs

**Hide-and-seek.** A child or children can carry treats and go hide while an adult holds the dog and covers his eyes. When the dog is released and finds a child, he gets a treat. It's great for the children to ask the dog to sit before giving him the treat, so the dog learns good manners and not to jump on the kids.

**Chase the toy.** An adult ties a squeaky or plush toy onto a 6-foot (2-m) cord or leash. The children take turns dragging the toy by the leash, while the dog chases

↑ **Preparing a dog for a new baby should start long before the baby is born.**

First, they had to decide if Molly would be allowed in the baby's room. If she was going to be allowed in the baby's room, they did not want her on the furniture, in the crib, or on the changing table. They started to teach Molly to go to her bed on cue. They worked on this trick not only in the nursery but also everywhere else in the house. They stationed several comfy dog beds in the areas of the house where they would be spending most of their time. Using treats and praise, they taught Molly to go to the nearest bed with the verbal cue "go to bed," and Molly learned to settle there until Mike or Mary gave her something else to do. Many times, they gave her a treat-filled toy or a chew toy while she was on the bed.

If Mike and Mary had decided not to allow Molly in the nursery, they could have taught her to go to her bed just outside the nursery door, or they could have replaced the nursery's regular door with a screen door. That way, Molly could still see and hear Mike and Mary in the baby's room and wouldn't feel as excluded as she would have if the solid door had been closed.

# What They Did Right

- Mike and Mary socialized and trained their adopted puppy, starting when she was very young.

- They taught Molly basic manners, such as staying at the bottom of the stairs and waiting at the door and before getting out of the car.

- They prepared the nursery and then started training Molly for her role in the baby's life.

- They prepared Molly for the baby by showing her a toy "baby" with all of the smells and noises that come with a baby. They taught her to be gentle and calm around the doll.

- They prepared Molly to expect changes in her daily schedule of meals, exercise, and playtime.

- They planned and practiced being positive when the baby was in the room with Molly.

↑ **Exchanging the regular door on the baby's room for a screen door will keep the puppy from feeling excluded when you are tending to the baby.**

The couple kept up with Molly's other training, like Down and Stay. They taught Molly to stay at the bottom of the stairs until they called her to come up, so she wouldn't be racing up the stairs, possibly tripping someone who was carrying the baby.

Mike and Mary borrowed a doll that made baby noises, and they bought some of the diaper cream and baby lotion that they planned to use with the new baby. By practicing with the doll, Molly could experience the noises and scents of a baby and get used to what Mike and Mary looked like when carrying the doll.

They made sure Molly got some exercise each day, but they encouraged her to retrieve toys so someone could play with her even if the baby was nearby. They practiced her tricks every day, but they also spent some time away from Molly, so she could start to understand they were not as available to her as they had been. It wasn't that Molly wouldn't get attention, playtime, love, and cuddle time, but it would be on a different schedule, and they wanted to get her used to the changes.

- They practiced praising Molly when she was gentle and calm around the doll.
- They taught her to sniff the doll and then go to her bed.

## George

A couple found George, a small terrier, in a trash heap, filthy, skinny, and covered with fleas. The couple decided to keep him, so they started on the work of cleaning him up, getting him healthy, and eventually having him neutered. House-training was tricky, but they got it done.

George was about ten months old and turned out to a be bit feisty, barking at strangers and other dogs. The couple quickly found out he wasn't good with small children, growling and snarling at them. Around the same time, they found out that they were expecting a baby themselves. Because they did not want to give up George, they basically divided their home to accommodate George's needs and allow for a child to grow up safely around him.

Strategic placement of baby gates, with George safely living in the lower level of the house, allowed him to spend time with the couple when the child was in bed. This worked out fine, and when the little boy was about three years old, George decided he was OK. While the child and the dog still always needed to be supervised, the family was able to incorporate George into the family's daily living.

↑   A doll scented with the lotion you plan to use on your new baby will help your dog
get used to baby smells.

- They praised and rewarded her for not jumping up on them or any visitors.
- They played a CD with crying baby sounds on it, gradually increasing the volume so Molly became used to it and was rewarded for her calm behavior.
- If Molly showed any concerns, they acted matter-of-fact about it and played with Molly to help her understand there was nothing to worry about.
- They changed her feeding schedule from having food available at all times to feeding her two meals a day. However, they varied the schedule randomly so Molly wouldn't get concerned if the meal was early or late.
- They agreed that they would never scold Molly in the presence of the baby. Everything about the baby would be fun, calm, and positive for Molly.

The next thing Molly knew, Mary was gone for a few days and then came home with the new baby. Molly took it all as a usual day, even though there was a lot of company and excitement in the house. She had already seen it all, smelled it all, and experienced it all, so there were no big surprises for her.

A year later, Molly was two years old, and the baby, Anna, was a year old. Molly's life was very different. Anna was starting to walk and talk, which could be scary for Molly.

Fortunately, Mike and Mary continued to train and socialize Molly to help her understand toddlers, which appear very different to dogs as soon as they start to crawl and then walk. They are about eye level with many dogs, and they stumble, cry, and speak a strange language. They like to grab tails, ears, paws, and noses.

Mike and Mary did a great job supervising Molly and Anna, even putting Molly in another room or outdoors if they couldn't supervise them. They also taught Molly to tolerate the occasional ear tug or tail grasp by performing these behaviors themselves, pairing the discomfort with treats to help Molly cope.

# DID YOU KNOW?

A dog that hurts a child is in danger of losing his home and his life—even if it is determined that the child or parent is at fault. Dog owners must be very proactive with anyone who wants to interact with their dog, even to the point of refusing if the dog is nervous, fearful, or uncomfortable.

# 7 House-Training: It's Easier than You Think

House-training is critical and an immediate concern. Any amount of time you spend on house-training is time well spent. The first few weeks of owning a puppy or dog are some of the hardest and the most important. Extra time and effort from the outset will pay off in a big way later.

The goal of house-training focuses on preventing accidents instead of waiting for them to happen. It is about making it easy for your dog to do the right thing in the first place. Training in this way takes a positive approach and is faster and more effective than correcting mistakes after the fact.

You play the most important role in the success or failure of your dog's house-training, as you must be patient, determined, and consistent for it to work. Whether you've adopted a puppy who's not yet house-trained or an adult dog with house-training problems, you can use the method presented here.

## DID YOU KNOW?

- Adult dogs can be house-trained in the same manner as puppies.

- Puppies have limited bladder control.

- Dogs and puppies like to be clean and to sleep in a clean area.

- All dogs do best when kept to a routine schedule.

↑ **Be proactive in taking your pup out often, even if he's not giving you signals.**

## Your Dog's First Night Home

When you first bring your adopted puppy or dog home, attach his leash and lead him or carry him from your car to the yard. Stay with him on the grass until he goes potty. When he does, tell him how wonderful he is. Bring him inside and play with him so he feels comfortable in his new surroundings.

Continue to take him outside at least every two hours while he is awake. Don't wait for him to make the first move.

Feed your dog in his crate. Afterward, put on his leash and lead him or carry him outside to potty before you do anything else. With a puppy, it is important to always carry him outside as soon as you open the crate. Puppies seem to have a urinating "reflex" that kicks in the moment they step out of their crates. If you let him walk to

### Training Tip

Even if you have a fenced yard, you must stay outside with the puppy or dog until he does his business. He won't understand what you are trying to teach him if you leave him alone in the yard.

the door, he will no doubt have an accident before he gets there. Part of this training is psychological. You want him to feel grass, not your floor, under his feet when he goes to the bathroom.

Once outside, wait for your dog to have a bowel movement before returning inside. Some dogs handle this job quickly, while others take longer to accomplish their task. Start using a verbal cue, such as "hurry up." Act happy when you have success.

After another short play period, take the dog outside again and then tuck him into his crate for the night. Place the crate near your bed so if he cries during the night, you can take him outdoors to potty. After he relieves himself outdoors, put him back in the crate. If you play with him, he may decide that it is playtime, not sleep time.

## Creating a Daytime Schedule

Establish a regular schedule of potty trips, playtimes, and feedings. This helps you control the times he goes outside and helps prevent accidents in the house. Here is a sample schedule that you can modify for your own needs:

# DID YOU KNOW?

Dogs have to go potty:
- When they wake up in the morning or after a nap
- Shortly after eating and drinking
- Before they go to sleep
- After stressful events
- After, and sometimes during, active play

If a dog, and especially a puppy, is not allowed to relieve himself at these times, he likely will have an accident. Be proactive. Don't wait for the dog to "tell" you that he has to go out. Assume he does and take him outside.

## Training Tip

Whether you carry or lead your dog outside to potty, always have him on leash. This way, you can keep him in his designated potty area, and you can keep him close to you so you can make sure that he goes and can praise him when he is successful.

- **Morning:** Immediately carry or lead the dog outside to potty. Let him play indoors for about an hour in the same room where you are.
- **Breakfast:** Feed the dog in his crate. About half an hour after he has finished eating, carry or lead him outside to potty. Stay with him outside and give him enough time to have a bowel movement.
- **Playtime:** Let the dog play indoors for an hour or so, but supervise him and don't give him free run of the house. Use baby gates or closed doors to keep him out of rooms that he shouldn't explore. Dogs of all ages are notorious for using out-of-the-way corners as bathrooms. If you give your dog too much freedom too soon, he will make a mistake.
- **After playtime:** Take him outside again and then put him in his crate for a nap.
- **Repeat:** Follow the same schedule of mealtimes, playtimes, and nap times throughout the day, taking him out to potty after each of them. Keep in mind that a puppy will start off with three or four meals a day, while an adult dog typically eats twice a day. With a puppy, you can lengthen playtimes as he gets older and more

↑   **Give your dog supervised indoor playtime in between potty trips.**

reliable. Eventually, your dog will let you know when he needs to go out. Don't ignore his request or take too long to get him outside, or he will have an accident. Instead, set him up for success.

We know that keeping to a strict schedule sounds like a lot of work, and, honestly, it is. But the results will pay off in a house-trained pet and clean carpets. Ideally, you are reading this before you bring your new puppy or dog home. If not, just pick up the schedule at an appropriate place for your situation.

In addition to your efforts, a lot of your dog's success will depend on how he was raised and trained before you adopted him. If he was not trained properly, be patient. You can train him. It will just take a bit longer.

Consider using the "umbilical cord" method when your dog has free time in the house. Use a soft buckle collar and leash that connect you to the dog. This helps prevent accidents because you always know where your dog is.

## House-Training with a Crate

As we've previously mentioned in the example potty schedule, house-training calls for the use of a dog crate, or at least a small confined area for the pup to stay in when he can't be supervised. Think of the crate as your dog's private room, where he can rest and stay safe and secure, away from trouble (such as chewing your furniture) and danger. A crate will make the task much easier, but a small area will also work.

For a puppy, you might want to use a crate divider (most crates come with them) to block off part of the space in a larger crate during house-training. You don't want the puppy to think he can potty in one end and sleep in the other or, even worse, learn not to care if there is a mess in the crate. If you have purchased a crate for him to "grow into," use the divider to reduce the inner space while he is small.

If you must leave your puppy or a small dog at home unsupervised, try using a different setup to help him successfully potty outside of the crate. Place the crate in

# Accidents
## Possible Reasons for Accidents

Feeding issues, changes in diet, health problems, and emotional upsets (a new pet or a new family member) can cause your puppy or dog to have accidents.

**Feeding:** Almost all dog food packages suggest feeding guidelines, but your dog may need less than suggested. Puppies often eat more than they need because they like the taste of the food. If you have a puppy that is producing more than three or four stools a day, try cutting back the food a little and using a measuring cup to feed consistent portions. Your veterinarian can help you monitor the pup's growth and condition.

Be sure that you are feeding an optimal-quality food. If the first few ingredients listed are mostly grain, such as corn, oats, or rice, you might consider changing to a food with meat products, such as chicken or lamb, among the first three ingredients. *Meal* means meat that has been ground and dried; generally, it is a good product. *Meat by-products*, however, can be nearly anything left in the rendering process and are not necessarily beneficial as food ingredients.

↑   If given too much freedom, your puppy is likely to find an out-of-the-way corner to do his business when he's ready.

## Troubleshooting

Puppies, especially those younger than three months old, have limited bladder control and reflexes. They can't predict that they need to "go" until the critical moment. Therefore, if you have a young puppy, it is not realistic to expect him to let you know ahead of time. If you are observant, you will notice that a puppy looking for a place to go potty will circle about while sniffing the floor, and you can get him outside quickly. The sniffing is instinctive—he is looking for a place that has already been used. If he can't find one, he'll make one. By preventing accidents inside, you'll teach him that the only appropriate bathroom is outside.

Changing your dog's food or giving him too many treats or table scraps can cause diarrhea. If you do change brands, do it gradually by mixing the old and new foods for several days. A change in water supply can cause problems, too. If you are moving or traveling, take along a couple gallons (8 or so liters) of water from home to mix with the new.

**Health problems:** Diabetes in adult dogs and urinary-tract infections in both dogs and puppies are common and can cause frequent urination. Such infections are common in female puppies. A symptom is frequent or unpredictable squatting with little urine release. A dog with a urinary tract infection will not display the usual behavior of sniffing, circling, or going to the door. Sometimes, the dog simply cannot make it outdoors. If you suspect this or any type of physical problem, check with your veterinarian. With a urinary tract infection, simple antibiotics take care of the problem, and then it's back to a normal potty schedule. Other medical problems may require further veterinary attention.

## Troubleshooting

What if your dog goes potty while you are gone? Try one or more of these options:
- Change his feeding schedule.
- Do a double potty trip outdoors before you leave him.
- If he goes potty because of anxiety, talk to a dog behavior expert about options.
- Check out doggy daycare.
- Ask a friend or neighbor to come in during the day for a walk or potty time.

↑ **Don't scold a puppy for having an accident indoors. Instead, be more vigilant in supervising him and getting him outside quickly.**

**Freedom:** Another problem we find when pet owners are frustrated with house-training is that they are giving the new puppy or dog too much freedom. As previously suggested, keeping a leash on the dog in the house can make the difference between an accident and a successful trip to the door.

**Dirty conditions:** If you've adopted a dog who has been raised and kept without the benefit of house-training, such as a neglect, kennel, or breeding situation, you might want to contact shelter staff or a trainer with experience in tougher cases to help you through the process. It may take this dog some time to adapt to a clean environment, so modifications to the "normal" house-training routine might help.

## Preventing Accidents

The method of house-training outlined in this chapter, using a crate and paying attention to schedules, feeding, and freedom, is based on preventing accidents. If you are diligent in taking your dog outside often enough, you will get fast results. If your puppy makes a mistake because you did not get him out when you should have, it is

If you catch the pup in the act of having an accident, stay calm. Make a startling noise, such as clapping your hands, to try to stop the action, and then carry him outside to his usual spot. As you set him on the ground, tell him "go potty" and praise him when he finishes the job.

## Cleaning Up Accidents

Potty accidents will invariably happen. If your puppy or dog has an accident, put him out of sight while you clean up. Cleaning a hard floor is fairly simple. For carpeting, get a lot of paper towels and keep blotting until you have lifted as much liquid as possible. Don't use a cleaner with ammonia, as that will attract the puppy or dog back to the scene of the accident. Instead, choose a product from the pet-supply store that will neutralize the ammonia, not just mask the odor. In a pinch, dilute white vinegar 1:1 with water.

Remember that dogs are attracted to urine odors, and their noses are much better than ours. They can pick up even the tiniest residue from commercial odor-killing products. Keep an eye on any spot where your dog has had an accident to make sure he doesn't use it again.

## Tips for House-Training Older Dogs

If you are trying to train an adult dog that is having house-training problems, start from the beginning with a modified puppy schedule and a crate. An adult dog can be expected to control himself for longer periods if you take him outside at critical times—first thing in the morning, after meals, and right before bed. Get him outside every three to four hours between those times.

An adopted adult dog that has been used to the freedom to potty off leash outdoors might not have a bowel movement when on a leash. Walk him a little longer, use a longer leash, or keep him confined until he really has to go. More freedom in the house comes with more reliability.

Make sure that your dog is really done before taking him back indoors. The process is a little trickier with an adult dog because you can't just scoop him up and take him back outside. Use a leash to take him out as needed.

# 8 Basic Training and Cues

In this chapter, you will learn how teaching your dog self-control and manners using our Nothing in Life Is Free training system can make everyday living with your dog enjoyable for him and everyone in the home.

Your dog will learn to:

- Sit quietly while you put on his leash
- Stay and wait for permission to go through any door
- Sit politely to be petted by friends in your home or by strangers on the street
- Give up something he has stolen because you have taught him to trade
- Back away from something dangerous on the floor or the sidewalk because you have taught him to leave it

We encourage you to start training as soon as you bring your new dog home. Enroll him in classes. Keep working with him and teaching him. You will soon discover how many wonderful things your dog can learn.

Consistency among all family members is key when training your dog. To avoid confusing the dog and frustrating the humans, we encourage all family members to use the same verbal cues, hand gestures, tone of voice, and body language when training him.

↑ **Start working on basic exercises right away with your newly adopted puppy or dog.**

## Nothing in Life Is Free

We have been teaching the Nothing in Life Is Free training method at the ARL for many years. It is the foundation for all of our training. In brief, the dog learns that when he behaves the way we want him to behave, he will always be rewarded for the desired behavior. For example, your dog learns that Sit gets him a favorite treat or another reward. If your dog wants to go for a walk, he knows that he has to sit quietly while you put his leash on. He knows that if he jumps, squirms, or does anything but sit, you will put the leash away. You may return and try again in a few minutes, but, if the dog does not immediately perform the desired behavior you've requested, he must wait for his walk.

This training system is not a magic pill that will solve a specific behavior problem. Rather, it is a way of living with your dog that will help him behave better. He trusts and accepts you as his leader, and he is confident knowing his rules and boundaries in your family. He learns that when he behaves, he receives something good.

In summary, with Nothing in Life Is Free, you will:

- Always use positive-reinforcement training to teach your dog
- Teach your dog cues for good manners and a few tricks

- Practice
- Only reward your dog when he performs the desired behavior according to your cue

# Training Self-Control

One of the first things to train any dog is self-control. You may have seen puppies that move randomly and frantically, chew anything in reach, or bark and whine to get attention. Puppies may even resort to growling or snarling— behaviors often associated with food, bone, or toy guarding—or they may nip when handled or restrained.

At the shelter, we see many teenage dogs (four to eighteen months) with handling issues. They have learned that frantic jumping and running can get them a chase game, that a growl or snap will get them released, or that grabbing toys and shoes garners attention. When that attention is scolding, it may not be the attention that they want, but it *is* attention.

Without proper training, inappropriate behaviors continue and become more and more challenging to correct. It is so easy for an owner to react. If the owner responds

↑　**With this training method, good things come to well-behaved dogs.**

every time the dog whines by asking him why he is upset, the dog quickly learns that whining gets attention. This can lead to a very whiny dog.

Likewise, if you allow your cute, small puppy to jump up for attention, he will continue, and when that same puppy is a 50-pound (23-kg) adolescent, you'll find that jumping up is no longer cute. We encourage owners to take every opportunity to reward good behavior early and build on that to teach self-control. Here's how to start.

## Training—Session 1

Begin training at mealtime. When owners leave the food bowl out, allowing the dog to eat whenever he wants, it can complicate house-training efforts as well as give the dog the idea that food is free and has no strings attached to humans. It can also make using treats for training much less effective. So, we suggest that you begin training self-control using the food bowl as a teaching tool.

Put food in the dog's food bowl as usual and get his attention while you are holding the bowl. If your dog knows the cue for Sit, use it just once to help him understand what the game is about. If he doesn't yet know the Sit cue, stand patiently, holding the food bowl over his head until he stops jumping up, running around, or whatever else he is doing and quiets down.

In this instance, the food bowl is being used as both the cue and the lure (reward) for your dog to sit. Cue your dog to Sit by slowly moving the food bowl back over his forehead. He should be watching the food bowl. Give the verbal cue "sit" just once. When the dog sits, put down the food bowl.

In summary:

1. Hold the food bowl just over your dog's head so he's watching it.
2. Using the food bowl, cue your dog to sit by slowly moving the food bowl over his forehead.
3. When the dog is sitting, lower the food bowl.
4. Put the bowl down and let him eat.

↑  **A simple behavior, such as sitting before eating, reinforces manners and builds self-control.**

If, after a few minutes of standing patiently and holding the food bowl, your dog hasn't yet sat down, put the food bowl away and repeat again later, waiting until he is sitting before lowering the bowl to feed him.

You can teach this self-control behavior in other areas of your dog's life, such as petting, leash walks, going in and out of doors, and any other time that you would prefer him to sit instead of demand.

## Training—Session 2

At the next session, repeat the same scenario. Give the Sit cue one time only and then stand there with the bowl, waiting for the Sit. When your dog does sit, and you start to lower the bowl, he will likely stand or jump up. Stand straight back up with the bowl, without saying a word, and wait for the dog to sit again. Chances are, he will sit much quicker this time, but it could still take a few minutes.

Waiting while your dog figures out on his own how to get you to lower the food bowl is worth the patience it takes on your part. Over the next few meals, he will start to anticipate your lowering the bowl and will stay calm or sit before you ask. If he doesn't or forgets, just stand still and let him think about it. Dogs learn so much

↑ **Jumping up is not polite behavior, whether for attention or food.**

better when we let them figure out how to do what we want, which to them is all about getting what they want.

**You can get your dog used to you handling his food bowl by hand-feeding him a few pieces of food from the bowl.**

### Training—Session 3

To advance to the next level, your dog not only has to sit while you lower the bowl, he also needs to stay sitting until you release him to eat. For this, you will need the Sit cue and a release word. Most people use "OK" as a release word. Use the same process as in the previous sessions, but this time, if the dog sits and then stands or jumps forward to eat, pick the bowl back up. Each time he raises his rear to get up before you say "OK," pick up the bowl. Quickly, he will learn that sitting and staying in that Sit position until he hears "OK" gets him his meal.

Resist the temptation to take back the bowl after you have said "OK" and released your dog to eat. This

↑ **When the dog is looking up at the food bowl, it's easy to lure him into a Sit.**

will seem like teasing to the dog and may cause him to start guarding the bowl from you, even to the point of threatening you. At the very least, it could cause him to hurry to eat his meal, which may not be healthy. Once you've released the dog to eat, let him eat.

## Training Sit Using Cue/Lure and Reward

The goal is for the dog to sit quietly with his tail and hindquarters on the floor. There are three progress levels when training Sit.

**Level 1:** Luring the Sit behavior and giving the lure as a reward.

**Level 2:** Using a hand signal (cue) for Sit but rewarding from somewhere else.

**Level 3:** Adding a verbal cue and proofing the behavior with distractions.

## Defining the Terms

**Cue hand:** The hand that gives the hand signals

**Lure:** The treat

**Lure hand:** The hand that holds the treats (lures)

**Lure/cue hand:** The hand that gives the hand signals while holding the treats

**Jackpots:** An offering of five or more treats at one time to reward the dog when he does especially well. For example, if you are working on Sit, and he immediately sits the first time you use a verbal cue without a hand signal, give him several of his favorite treats. He will remember what he did to get those treats and work to repeat that behavior.

When offering a jackpot, some trainers dispense the treats one at a time in succession and others reward with all five at once. Determine what works best for your dog. Also, don't offer jackpots too often, or they will no longer be special.

## Level 1

At Level 1, a hand over the dog's head tells the dog to sit. You use only the lure/cue hand to signal and treat. Do not say "sit" or say your dog's name, just reward him with the treat and offer praise each time he follows the cue. Use quiet, calm praise, because you don't want him to get excited and stand up when he is sitting. Resist the urge to say "sit" even if your dog already knows the verbal cue for Sit. You are training a technique as well as a behavior, and once your dog understands the cue/lure/reward technique, you can teach him many behaviors using just this method. But, in the beginning, we want to be silent until we are sure the dog understands that a hand over his head means Sit.

Have at least ten treats per session ready in a bag, bowl, or your pocket. Keep two or three in your lure/cue hand so you can quickly deliver them to your dog. Also remember to praise your dog each time he is successful. The rest of the time, stay silent.

Practice this behavior at least three times in sets of ten. Count out ten treats, use them as a set, and repeat the set three times.

If you start to get frustrated and need to take a break, toss a treat to the side of the dog for him to get "for free" and restart later. One of the amazing things about dogs

↑ **At Level 1, give the treat from the same hand that lured the dog into Sit.**

is that even when we are sure they don't grasp what we are trying to teach, they often understand it quickly when you start over.

1. Start by standing upright with your dog on leash. Have treats ready.

2. Hold the treat in your lure/cue hand just over the dog's nose, eyebrows, or forehead.

3. When the dog makes the slightest effort to drop his hindquarters, give him the treat and praise. Watch him back toward his tail, not his head. If he sits right away, give him the treat and continue to give him all ten treats, one each second,

## Defining the Terms

**Treat:** Food reward. When training your dog, work with soft, tasty treats that are easy to carry and count out. You want to be able to do many repetitions and keep the dog's interest at the same time. You may need to have several types of your dog's favorite treats handy. You can use commercial dog treats, but also try Cheerios and pieces of other low-sugar cereals, cubes of cheese, or fat-free turkey hot dogs cut into very small pieces. Stay away from high-salt and high-sugar treats.

Try different treat options to see what your dog likes. Save his favorites for his best efforts and for jackpots.

unless he stands up. Giving several treats is the start of the Stay behavior and teaches the dog that staying in a Sit position will be rewarded.

*Note:* If you have a small dog, bending over him may be intimidating to him. If this is the case with your dog, kneel when teaching the Sit.

### Level 2

In Level 1, the treat is in the lure/cue hand. In Level 2, the treat comes from somewhere else. Now, you will have the treat in your other hand, in a pocket, or on a nearby counter. Don't rush to this level, but don't avoid it, either. When your dog is sitting readily at least four out of five times when you lure/cue with one hand, start putting the treat in your other hand. Now you are cuing the dog with the cue hand and getting the treats from the lure hand. Give treats with each correct result, but the treats come a bit slower because you have to reach to get them. Deliver the treat right to the dog's mouth so he doesn't have to get up or move to get it. That helps keep him in the sitting position.

# Troubleshooting

If your dog has figured out that the treat is not in your cue hand and won't sit, there is an intermediate level to help with the changeover.

Start with a treat in each hand, using your lure/cue hand as in Level 1, but when the dog performs, he doesn't get a treat from the lure/cue hand. Instead, reach to get the treat from your other hand. Your dog will learn that the treat comes anyway but with a tiny delay. If you practice this step a few times, you will be able to go on to the next step without the treat in your lure/cue hand.

You should be ready to start this level after just a few sessions of Level 1 with your dog. Use the same pattern of three sets of ten treats. Practice whenever you get a chance, ideally two or three times a day, but only a minute or two each time.

Be sure to verbally praise your dog as well as reward him. Eventually, you want your dog to work for your praise as well as the occasional treat. Pairing praise with food increases the value of the praise and helps the dog understand that he can enjoy a reward of praise only. This will help you during the many times when you will cue him to do something but don't have treats with you, and praise is the reward.

# Training Tips

If your dog starts to jump up instead of sit, you may be holding the treat too high over his head. Try keeping it closer to him. Each dog has a different target point that works best for him.

If your dog stands up, back up a step, encourage him to come to you, and start over. Backing up a step gives him a chance to stand in front of you again and allows you to reset the exercise.

## Level 3
### Adding a Verbal Cue

Now that your dog will quickly and willingly sit with a hand signal, it is time to add a verbal cue. Pick the word you want to use, and make sure that everyone in the household uses the same word. Most trainers recommend one-word cues; for Sit, the most obvious word is "sit."

1. Start with your ten treats in a treat bag or bowl nearby. Say your cue word or phrase and use your cue hand to signal one second after you say the cue. Your dog might look at you questioningly for a second or two, but resist the urge to repeat either the hand signal or the verbal cue. Just stand there and see what the dog does.
2. The first few times, he might hesitate to sit, but if he seems to be starting to sit, reward him for his try. After that, wait a few seconds after you give the verbal cue and let him do the Sit before rewarding him. Remember, the verbal cue might be confusing to the dog at first, so help him work through the change.
3. Continue to work through your set of ten and then give the dog a rest.

### Proofing the Behavior

To *proof* the behavior means to practice with distractions, such as people, other pets, different locations, and at different times of day. You should also start varying your body positions to help the dog learn that, no matter if you are sitting down, standing up, looking at him, or turning away, if you say "sit," it always means the same thing and will always be rewarded with praise and treats.

Start by training your dog on the other side of the room. While it seems simple to us, this one change can alter a dog's perception of the training. You may have to revert to a treat in the lure/cue hand for a few trials. Don't worry—you will quickly be able to progress back to the verbal cue.

Practice three sets of ten treats and then move out to the garage and do more. This training can be tough mental work for your dog. It seems to be as tiring as a good run or play session. In fact, you can teach new behaviors, including tricks, when you and your dog can't get outside for regular exercise.

## Repeated Verbal Cues

If you repeat the verbal cue, you will lose the effect of getting the dog to respond quickly. Repeated cues can become "white noise" and easy for the dog to ignore. It is also easy to start sounding more stern and gruff with each repetition. You want to keep the verbal cues soft, quiet, and interesting.

It may take six or more tries for your dog to start to understand that the location is not important and he can perform the behavior anywhere and get the same

↑ Training outdoors introduces many distractions of scent, sight, and sound.

Using ten treats at a time is a simple way to keep track of when to move on with your training. If your dog performs eight times out of ten, move on to the next level. If not, stay at the same level until your dog can get at least eight out of ten right. You will use this method of keeping track with all of the behaviors we train.

rewards from you. This is called *generalization*. The more you change locations and add distractions to your training, the stronger the cues and results will become.

*Note*: Your dog does not need to be on a leash when you train in the house, as he should be eager to stay and interact. However, when you move outdoors, keep him on a leash or in a fenced area, safe from distractions.

## Training Down

Very often, owners teach their dog to sit but get stuck on trying to teach the Down behavior. It's harder to get a dog to do the Down for us, but to teach this behavior, we will follow the same pattern we used for Sit.

The goal is for the dog to lie down quietly with his body on the floor. There are three progress levels when teaching Down.

**Level 1:** Luring the Down behavior and giving an immediate reward.

**Level 2:** Using the hand signal to get the Down behavior and giving the treat from your other hand.

**Level 3:** Adding a verbal cue and proofing the behavior with distractions.

*Note*: Whether your dog is large or small, the process is the same with the exception that we recommend you kneel for a small dog and stand for a large dog.

## Level 1

To make this simpler for you and your dog, we reward the dog's incremental or tiny bits of effort.

1. Start with your dog sitting. Don't forget to continue to reward the Sit behavior. Using your lure/cue hand, take the treat and show it to the dog. Slowly drop your hand to the floor, keeping the treat in front of the dog.
2. Usually, the dog's nose will follow your hand with the treat. His shoulders will start to move, and his elbows will drop, even if it is just a little bit. If the dog lowers his body at all, slip him the treat and praise. Each time you lure him toward the floor, wait just a little bit longer as he lowers to the floor to give the treat.
3. Most dogs will lie down in two to four tries because it is easier to get the treat, and the crouching position can get uncomfortable.
4. For some small dogs, you may work with him under your bent knee (or under

↑ **A smaller dog may feel more comfortable if you kneel down to his level.**

the rungs of a chair). To do this, use your lure/cue hand and encourage the dog to follow it under your knee. Your goal, and the behavior you want to reward, is the dog lowering his shoulders to prepare to crouch. If your dog will lower his shoulders to follow the treat under your knee, reward him with a treat three or four times and then try it without using your bent knee. You can also use this technique with large dogs because the goal is not to get the dog under your knee but rather to get the dog into a crouch position so you can reward him. If you are still having trouble with this behavior, move on to another and come back to it.

## Level 2

You have been practicing using a lure/cue to get your dog to lie down and are probably taking the treat straight to the floor. In Level 2, the treat will come from a different location.

1. Hold one treat in your lure/cue hand and put ten treats in your other hand, the lure hand.

2. Give the same cue signal as in Level 1: the treat in your lure/cue hand and leading your dog into a Down position. Using your lure/cue hand, reach to your other hand and get a treat. Quickly give the treat directly to your dog, hopefully before he gets up. If he does get up, try to give him the treat as close to the floor as possible.

3. When your dog is successfully following your lure/cue hand with the treat you have been holding, give him the same cue without the treat. You will need to be quick

## Troubleshooting

If you have tried over and over, and your dog just won't lie down, look for why he may be reluctant. Maybe the floor is slippery or uncomfortable, or maybe there are distractions in the room.

Try varying the placement and movement of your hand as you lower the treat. Try faster, slower, farther ahead of the dog, or closer to the dog. One of these positions should start to work.

If you have a small dog, you might want to work on a low table or a bottom stair. This will enable you to put the treat below the level of the "floor" and encourage your dog to lie down. If you get a "shoulders down" but "tail in the air" position, reward it once. During the next try, wait to reward a full lying-down position.

about getting the treat from your other hand, your pocket, or the counter (lure hand). You are building trust with the dog as he begins to understand that the treat will still be there, even though it may be delayed a few seconds and coming from another location.

When you are able to cue your dog to the Down position without a treat in your cue hand, start to minimize the downward motion of the cue hand signal. Our goal is to be able to give the hand cue for Down from a standing position without having to bend over as we do in Level 1 when we take the treat to the floor.

You will know if you are going too fast or if your dog doesn't understand when he sits instead of lies down or if he keeps looking away. When you can depend on your dog to lie down at least eight out of ten times when you give the signal, you are ready to move on.

## Level 3
### Adding a Verbal Cue

Now that you can give a hand signal to your dog while standing in front of him and he will lie down, it is time to add the verbal cue. If you aren't to this point, practice a bit more or seek a coach to help you and your dog.

1. Say the verbal cue and then give your hand signal. Your dog might be a bit confused the first few times, so be patient and wait for him to figure it out. Do not repeat verbal cues or hand signals more than once. If the dog is still confused, practice the hand signal a few more times and reward him for success before adding the verbal cue.

2. When the dog is comfortable with both signals, try just saying the verbal cue. Again, say it *once*. Don't repeat it, just wait. If your dog hesitantly guesses and is right, it is a good time for a special treat or a jackpot.

↗ **If your dog stops paying attention to the training, take a break and try again later.**

# DOG TAILS

## Creative Training

I had one ingenious student teach her Greyhound to lie down by rewarding her for it in her crate. She couldn't find a way to reward her any other place, but the dog always would lie down in her crate. So, starting with success and really good treats there, she could get her to start lying down in other spots. It is fairly typical of retired racing Greyhounds to be reluctant to lie down. Also, because they are more muscled in their hindquarters than most dogs, they usually sit on their own muscles instead of the bones of their hip. They are never encouraged to sit or lie down in their training for the track, so it takes patience and creativity to get these behaviors from these special dogs.

### Proofing the Behavior

Begin to practice your verbal cues with distractions. Start with easy ones, such as turning on the TV or moving to a different room. Be patient and work through this stage carefully. If your dog falters, chances are you have added too much too fast. If this happens, go back to the place where your dog was successful and restart the training.

# Training Stay Using Cue/Lure and Reward

Your goal in teaching Stay is for your dog to remain in one spot until you give him an end signal. The end signal can be any word; words commonly used are "done," "over," or "OK." When training Stay, use treats to reward the dog while he stays and also after you give the end signal. So, treat, treat, treat while the dog stays, then give the end signal to release the dog, and then treat again. It seems like a lot of treats at the beginning, but it helps the dog learn the difference between doing the behavior and ending the behavior. *Note*: When teaching Stay, always hide the treats in your pocket, treat bag, or hand.

There are three progress levels when training Stay.

**Level 1:** Getting the Stay behavior, giving an immediate reward, and proofing the behavior with simple distractions.

**Level 2:** Adding the hand signal.

**Level 3:** Adding the verbal cue.

## Level 1

Training Stay in a Sit or Down position is the same. Practice with both positions. Several techniques will work, so see which you like best for your dog.

1. Have a handful of treats and ask for a Sit.
2. As long as your dog stays in the Sit, deliver one treat at a time, approximately one second apart, right to his mouth, about ten times. Say the end signal, let him get up, and immediately treat. At this point, your dog doesn't know the behavior. You are standing in front of your dog, delivering treats as long as he stays put. Deliver the treats to his mouth. Do not call him to come to you for the treat, or you are training him to move out of Stay.

## Where's the Treat?

Many trainers and owners use treat bags, but some dogs become focused on the treat bags instead of concentrating on their owners. If you can be less predictable about where the treat comes from, your dog will tend to focus on you.

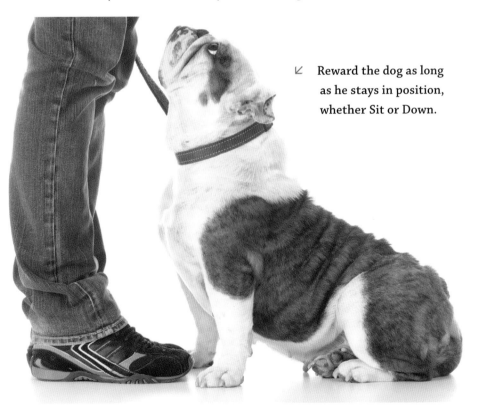

↙ Reward the dog as long as he stays in position, whether Sit or Down.

3. If your dog gets up and walks away, bring him back to the starting point and cue Sit. Follow the Stay procedure and treat, treat, treat. Chances are, your dog is sticking with you enjoying the "free" treats.

4. At the next session, start with the same procedure but add a small step to one side or the other before treating. Start very small. Treat while he stays. If your dog starts to come with you, stop the treats. Don't scold or frown at him; simply start over. Usually after two or three trials, your dog will figure out that if he stays put, he will get treats. He will begin to stay while you move. After delivering ten treats, say your end signal and walk a few steps away. You dog can't make a mistake when you say OK and he leaves the Stay. Deliver a treat.

## Level 2

In Level 1, your dog learned that if he stayed in one spot while you stepped to the side, he would get a treat. Now, you are going to add a hand signal and teach him to stay

↗ In the hand signal for Stay, your palm is facing the dog.

Be sure you don't push your dog too far too fast when teaching the Stay. Your dog will learn as much from his mistakes as from his successes. Several short sessions will work better than trying to work for an hour straight. If your dog is frustrated or bored, he will let you know by turning or walking away. If this happens, ask for a Sit or another successful and easy behavior and end your session. Try the Stay again after a little while.

During the Stay training program, go back to your dog to reward him. It is tempting to call him to you from a Stay position, but it is best to train Come as a separate exercise. This way, your dog doesn't start to anticipate the option to come and move out of his Stay.

for a span of time. The hand signal for Stay is generally a vertical hand with fingers up and the palm toward the dog, much like a "stop" signal.

After you are able to move several steps to the side, try walking around your dog. Add the hand signal. Treat. This can be difficult for your dog, and he may crane his neck to try to watch you. Keep a treat in front of his nose as you circle around him. He will learn that when you come back to face him, that is when he will get another treat.

Some dogs understand Stay quickly, while others don't understand why they should stay still while you move. Keep practicing, and when your dog is doing well in one location, move to another location to see if he has truly learned the behavior.

## Level 3

After your dog has learned the hand signal, add the verbal cue "stay." As before, say the new verbal cue before using your hand signal. Proof the Stay behavior by using it for short times around distractions, such as on your walks, in stores, and around the house. Be sure to reward your dog after you give the end signal.

# Training Your Dog to Come When You Call

Your goal is that your dog will come to you when you give the one-word verbal cue. Training your dog to come to you is a basic and essential command with many training options. Following is the method we have found most successful.

As with the previous exercises, there are three progress levels when training Come.

↑   **Always make coming to you a pleasant and rewarding experience for your dog.**

**Level 1:** Getting the Come behavior using the cue word and giving an immediate reward.

**Level 2:** Getting the Come behavior while moving around the room and cuing back and forth with another person.

**Level 3:** Proofing the behavior.

Decide on the cue word that you want to use when you call your dog. We suggest using the dog's name and the cue word "come." You will say the dog's name to get his attention, and she will look at you for the next instruction, which will be "come."

So, we are training the dog two things:

1.  Look at me when I say your name.

2.  Come to me when I say the cue word, "come."

Because the dog's name becomes very important in this exercise, you should be careful how and when you say it. You want him to associate his name with things he enjoys, like walks or dinnertime—so don't call him to come to you when you want to perform a task he doesn't like, such as clipping his nails. In these cases, just go to the dog, put his leash on him so he will come with you, and don't use his name.

## Level 1

Say your dog's name. When he looks at you, preferably making eye contact, present him with one piece of food directly to him mouth. You should be close to your dog when you begin so you can deliver the treat right away. Add your cue word, "come," after his name early in the training process because he will be responding quickly.

## Level 2

Repeat Level 1 with ten to twenty pieces of food, moving around the room, if necessary, to keep your dog returning to you. If someone else is available, split the food between the two of you and call your dog back and forth. Each time he comes to one of you, he gets one piece of food. The more people, the merrier, and the quicker the exercise goes. Plus, we are building lots of practice into this exercise. A round-robin game of "Rover, come" can get a quick response in just a few practices.

## Level 3

Begin to expect your dog to come to you, as well as sit politely once he gets there, before you present the food reward. Resist giving a verbal cue for Sit; instead, wait for him to guess. If he jumps up or wanders off, use his name again to get his attention. He will quickly learn that Come and Sit get him treats.

You want your dog to be consistent with this exercise so when you take it outdoors and add distractions, he will still respond quickly. When you do take this exercise outside, it is

← **Be close to your dog when you begin so you can deliver the treat right after you say "come."**

↑   Show one treat to your dog and close your hand.

↑   The dog will probably try to get to the treat in your hand.

## Level 2

After a few sessions, if your dog is doing well with Level 1, try using the treat in your open palm and presenting it to the dog. Be prepared to close your fingers over it if he tries to get the treat. He should quickly learn that this is the same exercise. The difference is that he can see the treat but still can't have it. As soon as he turns away from the treat in front of you or resists trying to get it, give him the treat from behind your back.

## Level 3

When you can show your dog a treat and predict that he won't try to get it, it is time to add a verbal cue. The common cue is "leave it.". To add the cue to the exercise, first say "leave it" and then present the treat in a closed hand as you did at the beginning of the exercise. We go back to the basics because we are changing things. You should be able to progress quickly once he understands that the cue "leave it" precedes a reward for leaving the treat in front of him.

Having taught a reliable Leave It using various interesting objects, like treats, toys, and even tissues, you should also be able to say "leave it" to your do when something is happening and you want him to stop in his tracks.

## Want to Trade?

Your goal is to have your dog drop something and get a treat. We often use it to teach a dog to drop a toy so we can throw it again. You can also use it to get your dog to drop anything you don't want him to be carrying in his mouth or chewing on.

Use treats and a toy or rawhide bone to teach the Want to Trade? behavior. You want your dog to be able to take the "trade" into his mouth and hold it.

There are two levels for this training.

**Level 1:** Getting the behavior.

**Level 2:** Adding a verbal cue and proofing the behavior.

↑   **Sadie is asked to trade her toy for a treat.**

↑   **Once she gives up the toy, she receives her reward.**

## Level 1

To start, get some treats and a toy or rawhide that your dog will take into his mouth and hold.

1. Start with the toy or rawhide in one hand and several small treats in the other. Show the toy to your dog and let him take one end of it, and then quickly show him the treat from the other hand. We usually start using a verbal cue right away because it works so quickly. The verbal cue we use is "want to trade?"

2. When your dog releases the toy, deliver the treat right to his mouth. After you repeat this a few times, he might refuse to take the toy and will instead hold out for the treats. This is when you want to escalate the attractiveness of the toy. You can switch it out for a better one or put a smudge of peanut butter or cheese on the end. Offer him the toy but hold on to the end, say the verbal cue, and offer a treat to trade.

3. After your last successful trade, let your dog have a double reward by giving him a treat and then giving him back the toy he traded for the treat and end your session.

After a lot of practice, your dog will be able to give up something as wonderful as a dead bird he finds on a walk when you use your verbal cue. By then, he definitely knows that something good will happen when he hears those words.

If you don't happen to be carrying treats with you, substitute a good scratch and lots of praise. When you get home, practice again a few times with really good treats. You want him to remember that it is worth his while to trade, even if there isn't always an immediate treat.

## Loose Leash Walking

Your goal is to teach your dog to walk calmly beside you. If you have a dog that chronically and constantly pulls on the leash when you are walking him, it is hard for you or the dog to enjoy the exercise. Try the following suggestions, and you will both look forward to your daily walks. If you have a puppy or adult dog with no previous leash-walking experience, you have the opportunity to teach him positive on-leash habits.

Dogs love to explore and sniff all things. If the interesting object is out of leash range, the dog will lean into the collar to get closer. Stop and hold the leash firm, without allowing any give, to prevent the dog from going where he wants to sniff. Wait until the dog backs up a step or turns to you before you allow him to go to the interesting object as a reward for loosening the leash.

There are some tools available that can make walking on a loose leash easier to train. One tool we often use to train loose leash walking is a head-halter type of collar called the Gentle Leader® (*www. gentleleader.com*). Many owners continue to use Gentle Leaders throughout their dogs' entire lives. The dog quickly learns that, when the owner brings out the halter, it means a walk.

There are different brands of head halters as well as body harnesses out there, and if you choose to use one, we recommend that you spend some time acclimating your dog to it before using it on a walk. The fit of the product can make a big difference in its comfort and how well the dog tolerates it, so work with a trainer to ensure the correct fit.

Do not use collars meant to choke, cause discomfort to, or threaten the dog. Choke, pinch, and prong collars only work using pain or the threat of pain when he pulls. This

↑   When walking on a loose leash, the dog walks calmly beside you.

↑   If the dog starts to pull in another direction, stop. Wait until the dog takes a few
    steps back and start walking again once the leash is loose.

**When you teach your dog:** When your dog wants to lead you off the path, stop, keep the leash taut, and wait until your dog takes a step back. Then, loosen the leash and continue your walk.

**When your dog teaches you:** You are walking your dog. He sees something he wants to sniff. It is off your path but, being the kind person you are, you step toward the dog. The leash loosens as you follow the dog to the interesting object. Good for the dog. He has just taught you!

can result in increased stress, and your dog may become fearful or anxious about his surroundings, including people and other dogs.

Be a Tree is one technique we use to teach a dog to walk nicely on a leash. This entails standing still as soon as your dog starts to pull on the leash. When the dog relieves the tightness on the leash, you move forward with your dog. This works best

↑ Jake is being introduced to the Gentle Leader® head halter.

↑ A body harness is another option that may be more comfortable for your dog.

if the leash is short and the dog has the opportunity to move only a foot or so (about 0.3 m) in any direction. If you use a longer leash, the communication with the dog is slower and not as effective.

## Crate Training Your Adopted Dog

You already know from our discussion on house-training that we recommend crate training as part of the process. We also recommend crate training to manage your new pet's access throughout your home while he's learning manners and self-control.

A crate is a useful tool that your pet can be happy in when properly introduced to it. You can use a crate for safe travel, a time-out place when your dog needs to calm down, your dog's "den" when you have a houseful of people who aren't all comfortable with dogs, or a way to keep your pet comfortable when he's in a home where pets aren't welcome. Whatever the reason, if you properly train your dog to use his crate, he'll be happy in it and you'll be glad to have it as an option when needed.

↑   **Blankets and toys make the crate a comfortable "den" for the dog.**

Your dog may learn to be comfortable in his crate quickly, or he may take longer to adjust to it. The dog's age, disposition, and experience are all factors. A puppy who has had no previous experience with a crate may take to it more easily than an older dog for whom a crate may have an unpleasant association (for example, a dog rescued from a puppy mill). Regardless, make every step of crate training pleasant, with treats and praise, and don't misuse the crate by confining your dog in it for too long and too often.

## Selecting a Crate

The most popular types of crates come in hard plastic or collapsible metal wire. They come in various sizes and can be purchased from most pet-supply stores. Invest in a sturdy, appropriately sized crate. If you have a puppy, buy a crate that will fit your dog at his adult size.

## Crate Training Tips

- Puppies under the age of six months should not stay in crates longer than four hours at a time.

- If the puppy is home alone—for example, while you are at work—arrange to come home for lunch or find a neighbor or friend who can take him out to potty during the day.

- If you are consistent in not letting your dog out of the crate when he whines during the training process, chances are if he whines at night, he really does have to go out to potty. Take him directly outside, let him do his job, and put him directly back into the crate. Do not give him playtime or cuddle time, or he will start waking you up every night.

- Never punish or scold your dog or bang on the crate to get him to stop making noise. It will stress him, frighten him, and reward him with attention (albeit negative attention) for his efforts.

- Dogs like schedules. Once you establish daytime and nighttime schedules, your dog will start to predict bedtime and crate time and may even enter the crate before you give the cue.

## Introducing Your Dog to the Crate

Place the crate in an area of your house where the family spends a lot of time. Put a soft blanket or towel in the crate. Talk to your dog in a happy voice as you bring him over to the crate. If you are using a metal crate with a sliding pan on the bottom, also put a thin rug or towel under the pan to reduce any rattling noises that could startle your dog when he first steps in. Make sure the crate door is open and secured so it won't hit your dog and frighten him.

At night, we recommend putting the crate in the bedroom of an adult, at least while the dog is getting used to it. Crating a dog away from the family will often cause him stress or anxiety, and he may whine, bark, howl, yodel, or bay. Once your dog gets used to being crated at night, you can begin moving the crate, a little at a time, to your preferred location. It is important to keep a puppy within hearing distance at night because he may need to go outside to potty.

Remember, the crate should always be associated with something pleasant. Put treats and toys in the crate so the dog has to walk in to get them. Let him become comfortable entering and leaving the crate. Do not force him to enter the crate; give him time to figure it out. It may take some time, but it will be very helpful later in your training. When the dog does stay in the crate, continue to give him treats by dropping them in the back of the crate. If he leaves the crate, no more treats. Wait a few minutes and start again.

## DID YOU KNOW?

By placing treats inside the crate but shutting the dog outside the crate, you will build his interest in the treats inside and make him want to enter the crate.

Try feeding meals in the crate and leaving the door open. When it's clear that the dog is comfortable in the crate, close the door while he's eating. Open it when he's finished, as long as he is not barking or whining. Gradually extend the time that you keep the door closed. Each time your dog eats a meal with the door closed, add a few minutes to the time he stays in the closed crate after the meal. If he gets stressed, barks, whines, or digs at the crate, shorten the time he's in the crate with the door closed—but never open the crate door while he is making noise.

Along the same lines, do not approach or release your dog while he is whining, barking, or digging at the door of the crate. You want him to learn that quiet, calm behavior brings humans to him, and barking or whining makes humans stay away.

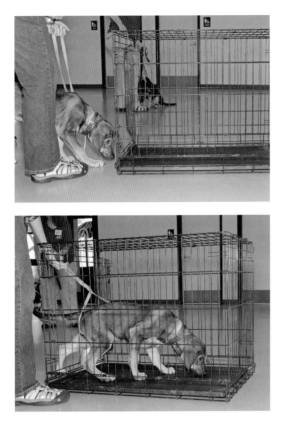

↖ Toss treats into the crate to encourage the puppy to enter. Never force him.

↑ Be sure the crate door is out of the way in case he backs up.

← Soon, the puppy will be entering on his own to get the treats. Keep practicing, gradually, to increase your pup's comfort level with the crate.

Crate train slowly, watching for fear, stress, or anxiety in your dog. If at any time you see him showing concern, back the training up to a place where he is comfortable, and stop. Continue later in the day, starting with the basics and quickly moving back to the spot where your dog showed stress.

Next, begin training your dog to go into the crate *before* you give the treat or set the food bowl down. Practice with him for about five pieces of food and then wait. Even if he takes just *one* step toward the crate, reward him by tossing the treat into the crate. He will start to figure out that if he goes in by himself, you will reward and praise him. Give him a *big* reward—multiple pieces of food or treats—for going in on his own, always putting the treats in the crate. Call him back out, but do not give him a treat. When you can look at the crate and he walks in, start putting a verbal cue with this behavior. Use words like "kennel," "in," "go to bed," or anything that makes sense to you.

Take the training a step further by giving your dog a treat, shutting the crate door, and walking out of sight. Come back to the crate before he starts to stress. Release him from the crate but do not give him a treat. Practice sending him to his crate and moving out of sight, but stay in the house. When he can stay in the crate calmly for ten minutes or so, go out the door by which you normally exit the house, count to five, and return. Be very calm and matter-of-fact when leaving and coming back in. We want this to become routine, even boring, for the dog. Repeat this process several times a day. With each repetition, vary the length of time you leave him. Don't be predictable. This may take several days or several weeks.

## Home Alone

When your dog can spend thirty minutes or so in the crate without becoming anxious or afraid, you can begin leaving him crated for short periods when you are away from the house. Crate him using your cue and a treat as a reward after he enters. You might also want to leave a toy in the crate but be sure the toy is something he can't chew into pieces while you are gone. Most dogs do fine with Kong® toys filled with treats or kibble. Have several Kongs prepared and in the freezer. Give one to your dog when you leave. He will stay busy getting the treats out as they thaw.

Leave and come home calmly. Only approach the crate if your dog is calm. If he has made a mess, don't scold or punish him, just take him outdoors as you normally do when you come home.

To aid in this training, crate your dog for short periods when you are home. You do not need to do this every day, just from time to time. You don't want your dog to associate crating with being left alone. The crate should be a bedroom, not a jail.

## Important!

Never put your dog in the crate for punishment or when you are angry with him.

# Rewarding and Reinforcing Behavior

By understanding the concept of *reinforcement*, you will see that you are not forever bound to carry a pocketful of treats. Your pet will soon be working for your verbal praise. He wants to please you, and he knows he will occasionally get a treat, too.

Take advantage of the many small opportunities to reinforce your dog's behavior. You may have him sit before letting him out the door, before petting him, or before giving him his food. Remember to always praise him and offer a treat when appropriate.

When your pet is learning a new behavior, you should reward him every time he does the behavior. This is called *continuous reinforcement*. It may be also necessary to use *shaping* with your pet. Shaping is the process of reinforcing something close to the desired response and gradually requiring more before giving the reward. For example, if you are training your dog to shake hands, you may initially reward him for lifting his paw off the ground, then for lifting it higher, then for touching your hand, then for letting you hold his paw, and finally for actually shaking hands with you.

You can start to use *intermittent reinforcement* once your pet has reliably learned a behavior. At first, you may reward him with the treat three times out of four, then about half the time, then a third of the time, and so forth, until you are only rewarding him occasionally with treats. Continue to praise him every time, though. Once he's learned the behavior, the praise can be a quiet, positive "good boy." Pairing the treats with praise early in the training makes the praise alone more effective.

## Clicker Training

The basic premise of clicker training is to teach the dog that the click means a reward is due. When you click for a desired behavior and then immediately reward your dog, he will try to repeat that behavior for more rewards. The click is the communication link that lets the dog know exactly what behavior earned him the reward. Often, by the time you say "good dog," your dog has already changed behaviors and may believe he is being rewarded for that behavior.

## Dog Facts

- Dogs can hear frequencies of 30,000 hertz (often higher); humans can only hear frequencies of up to 20,000 hertz. This means dogs can hear much higher-pitched noises than we can.

- A dog's sense of smell is up to 100,000 times stronger than a human's, depending on breed.

↗ The clicker fits in the palm of your hand and has a button to make the "click" noise.

So what does it mean to "click" a behavior? A clicker is a small handheld training tool, often a small plastic rectangle, with a button or metal bar that makes a clicking sound. When you click the clicker at the exact moment when your dog performs a desired behavior, and then follow the click with a treat, you are reinforcing and rewarding that behavior. You should always separate the click and the treat by about half a second. If you click and treat at the same time, the dog can become confused. Click first and then treat to make it clear to the dog. Proper timing is essential in clicker training.

You can also use clicker training to help a dog start a new behavior. An example might be training a dog to spin to the right. Use a treat to help the dog turn his head to the right and, when he does, click/treat. Repeat three to five times and click/treat each time. Then wait and see whether the dog will offer a head turn on his own. Be ready to click/treat him when he does. Soon the dog will be offering the head turn readily, so be sure to continue the click/treat.

Some people are concerned that they will need to carry a clicker forever. The clicker is used to start training and reinforcing new behaviors. Once the behaviors are on cue, you can phase the clicker out. The clicker is only the bridge to the reward. It signals to your dog "that was right, good dog, here's a reward."

Along with timing, an understanding of positive reinforcement is also essential to proper clicker training. Be sure that the reward you are using is actually rewarding to the dog. If your dog does not

## DID YOU KNOW?

If you click, whether you intended to or not, or you mistakenly clicked the wrong behavior, reward the dog anyway. Once you start clicker training, you want the dog to be very confident that a click equals a reward *every time*.

enjoy a pat on the head, he will not view it as a reward for his behavior. When you teach any new behavior, you will depend heavily on food as the primary reinforcer and the clicker or the phrase "good dog" or "yes" as the secondary, or conditioned, reinforcer. As the dog learns the behavior and its associated cues, whether verbal or physical, you will start to use the clicker less and praise more. Often, we start to randomly and variably reinforce the behavior.

If you choose clicker training, it may start with luring a Sit with a treat. When the dog's rear is heading toward the floor, click, and then quickly offer the food reward as the dog sits on the floor. After you have lured the Sit approximately five times and followed with click/treat, try standing still and see if the dog offers you a Sit. If he does, click and give a reward. If he doesn't, lure the Sit a few more times and try again.

Once the dog offers the behavior several times in a row, stop using a treat in the lure hand and keep the treats in your clicker hand. Your lure hand now becomes a cue behavior for the dog. Using the same gesture you did when you had the treat in your hand, see if the dog offers Sit. When he does, click and reward him. You have just taught a hand signal to your dog for Sit.

Whatever method you use, training should be enjoyable and fun for both the dog and the owner. We recommend encouraging your children to participate in the training, especially tricks, so they can show the dog off and enjoy practicing. Positive reinforcement in the form of treats and praise is key to all training, including clicker training.

## Clicker Training Info

For more information on clicker training, go to the website of clicker training expert Karen Pryor, *www.clickertraining.com*. It is easy to learn, and the whole family can participate by using this technique.

→ **When the dog hears the click, he will expect the reward to follow immediately.**

# 9 Your Healthy Dog

Usually we think we can tell if there is something wrong with our dogs. The concern is that many dogs cannot or will not spell out their discomfort. Check your dog over daily, looking for warm or cold spots, lumps, limping, hair loss, unusual or unpleasant odors, or anything that is different from what you have noticed before.

## Daily Health Checks

**Eyes and nose.** Look at your dog's eyes. If there is a discharge that isn't the normal, clear, tear-like discharge, start looking for other problems. Discharge that is thick and has a color can indicate an infection. Check his nose. Dogs have their noses everywhere and can be exposed to injuries, infections, or even weeds and seeds that can become lodged in the soft tissues. An itchy nose can indicate the start of an upper respiratory infection, an injury, or something else out of place.

**Coat and skin.** While you're petting your dog, look at his coat and skin. Hair loss and itchy skin are reasons to visit your vet. Hair loss, especially around the eyes and lips, can be the start of a skin infection. Many things can cause both symptoms, including allergies, ringworm, and mange mites, to name a few. While these symptoms do not constitute an emergency, you should get them checked by your vet for both the health and the comfort of your dog. If your dog sleeps with you and is itchy, you won't get much sleep, because he will be licking, scratching, and chewing off and on all night.

↑ Check your dog's eyes, nose, and coat regularly to catch any problems early.

To keep a healthy coat in good condition, bathe your dog as needed. Most dogs only need to be bathed every two to three months, unless they have rolled in something smelly. Brush your dog three to four times a week, no matter the length of his coat. This will get rid of dead skin and distribute the natural oils for a shiny coat and healthy skin. Brushing also helps minimize shedding.

**Lumps.** Do you see or feel any lumps on your dog's body? Lumps should always be checked by your veterinarian. With lumps, especially under the jaw, in the armpits, or on the belly, don't wait, thinking they will go away or get smaller. Have them checked while they are small in case they turn out to be something serious.

**Odor.** If you notice a distinctively smelly discharge or odor from your dog's rear end, it should be checked by your vet. It could be an infection or other problem with the anal glands, which can be painful for the dog. Butt-scooting or excessive licking of the tail, flank, or genital area can also signal anal-gland problems. Butt-scooting can also be caused by worms or fleas.

**Limping.** Limping is a concern but might not be an emergency unless you know for sure that your dog was injured. Always contact your veterinarian, who may

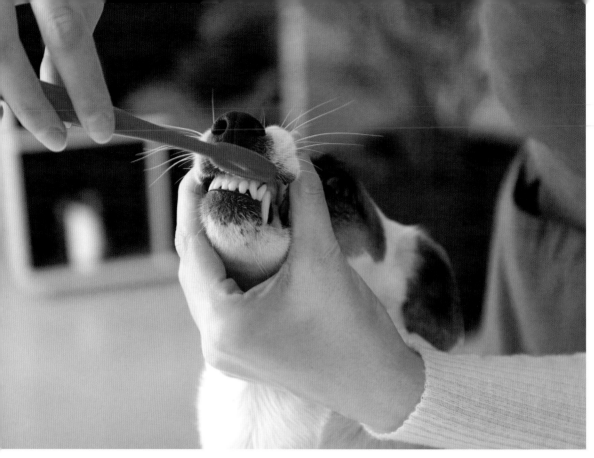

↑ **Brushing your dog's teeth at home can help prevent dental problems as he ages.**

recommend X-rays to diagnose the symptoms. In some young dogs, the limping may seem to change legs, moving from side to side or even front to back. This can be a painful condition called *panosteitis*, indicating "growing pains" or "wandering lameness."

**Gums and teeth.** During your daily check, look at your dog's gums and teeth, something he should be readily willing to let you do. Gums should be pink, but not pale pink and not bright pink. Check regularly so you know what his normal color is. Some dogs have black gums and even black or dark tongues, so noticing a change may be more difficult. The color can change with exercise, exposure to heat, injury, or disease. If you see a change in gum color, contact your veterinarian.

Any dog's teeth will yellow with age, but if you see tartar, which looks like dark layers of stuff building up on the gumline, talk to your vet about options. A dental scaling by your vet usually requires full anesthesia, so it's worth it to be proactive.

# Heartworm

According to the American Heartworm Society, *www.heartwormsociety.org*, most areas of the United States have cases of heartworm. The farther south you go, the greater the concentration of the infections. When we brought many dogs into rescue groups from Hurricane Katrina, it seemed as if nearly all of the dogs had heartworm.

Your dog's yearly physical exam will include a test to look for the presence of heartworms, which are carried by infected mosquitoes, in the dog's blood. If your dog is heartworm-free, your vet will suggest suitable preventive options for your dog. Preventive monthly treatments are effective and, depending on the brand, can also help keep your dog from being infected with other internal parasites, like hookworms and roundworms, which can both be infectious to humans as well as dogs. Work with your vet to find the best preventive for your pet. It's too risky not to be proactive in preventing heartworm. Heartworm treatment is very hard on a dog, not to mention expensive.

Ask your vet about other prevention ideas. Some dogs that regularly chew toys may have less tartar. Using a toothbrush and special canine dental paste can be a good way to go. Your dog may not enjoy it at first, so start slowly with the brush, doing a few teeth at a time. Many dogs like the taste of the doggy toothpaste and don't resist it, so you might have an easier time using a washcloth with the toothpaste. Try to work your way back to the large molars in the rear of his mouth. He may work against you

# When to Visit the Vet

Sometimes your pet just doesn't seem right. Maybe he has less of an appetite or he's not eating at all. Maybe he's moving more slowly or doesn't want to play ball or just seems grumpy. How do you know when there is something seriously wrong?

Call your veterinarian's office and ask the person who answers the phone. He or she has been specially trained to get information from you and help you decide what could be an emergency. Many things can wait until morning, but bleeding, injuries to eyes or internal organs, and broken bones cannot.

by making chewing motions with his jaws, so be careful where you put your fingers.

**Toenails.** Check your dog's toenails about every two weeks and clip them (or have them clipped) if needed. If you are comfortable clipping your dog's toenails, we find it is best to do it after a bath, as the toenails are soft and less likely to have sharp edges. If the dog is still in the bathtub, he may stand more quietly than if he were lying on the floor with you. Use nail clippers designed specifically for pets. Clip off just the tip of the nail, being careful not to nick the vein running through it.

**Ears.** Take a peek into your dog's ears each week. Sniff to see if there is a yeasty or unpleasant odor. If you notice this, be sure your veterinarian checks it to see what treatment will work best. Don't try to treat an ear infection without getting it diagnosed, as some of the over-the-counter remedies can make an infection worse or cause your dog pain instead of helping the problem. Use a cotton ball with ear cleaning solution or a baby wipe to clean the inside of your dog's ears. Do not force your finger or a Q-tip into the ear canal.

## Choosing a Veterinarian

The shelter gets many calls from dog owners who do not have a regular veterinarian, and we advise them about what to look for when choosing a veterinarian. When choosing a vet, you're not just evaluating the vet but the staff and clinic as well.

## Troubleshooting

I get questions from owners whose dogs have become aggressive "suddenly" or "out of the blue." My first suggestion is a veterinary check, because many times a sudden behavior change can have a basis in a medical issue. Old age or injury can cause a normally tolerant dog to suddenly be defensive or grouchy. There are some great medications that can help with pain and can keep dogs comfortable while they heal or if they are dealing with chronic pain, such as arthritis.

Look for a clean veterinary facility with a welcoming reception area.

# First-Aid Situations

Would you know what to do if your pet was bleeding or choking? In some emergencies, you can help your pet before getting him to the veterinarian. We recommend looking into pet first-aid classes offered by the American Red Cross (*www.redcross.org*). Also refer to the First-Aid Kit section on page 67 for a list of the first-aid supplies you should have on hand.

- **Friendliness.** The staff should greet you by name when you walk in the door, or they should at least know your dog's name.
- **Cleanliness.** If you walk into the waiting room and something smells bad or looks dirty, be concerned. Much of veterinary medicine is done in sterile conditions, and if the lobby and exam rooms are not kept clean (not necessarily sterile), chances are the rest of the clinic is not clean.
- **Focuses on the dog and you.** In addition to being friendly and personable, the staff and veterinarian should treat you and your dog as their only concern during your time together.
- **Lets you stay with your dog.** You may want to be able to stay with your dog during the exam and vaccinations, but some clinics routinely remove the dog from your presence to the back of the clinic for shots and toenail trims. If you want to stay with your dog during all procedures, make your preferences clear.

# Healthy Dogs, Healthy Owners

Good hygiene and maintaining our pets' good health will prevent us from catching diseases or parasites from them. All dogs should be routinely examined for internal and external parasites. For example, dogs can harbor roundworms, parasites that can infect people and cause skin problems, blindness, or organ damage. People with decreased immune function can be more at risk of catching something from a family dog, and such people should always consult with their doctors before adopting a pet. For more information about zoonotic diseases (diseases that can be passed to humans from animals), check the American Veterinary Medical Association's website at *www.avma.org*.

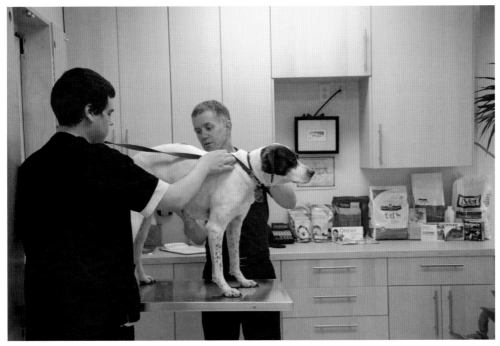

↑ **Look for a vet clinic with doctors and staff who are knowledgeable, friendly, and skilled at handling pets.**

- **Gets down to the dog's level.** Will the vet techs and the veterinarian get down to your dog's level if he is not comfortable on an exam table? In what other ways does the staff and vet work to make visits easier for nervous or fearful dogs?
- **Tells you your options.** Before treatment, a good vet will tell you all of your options. Will there be different treatment options if they do more tests? Does the cost of more testing become a factor if the condition is serious? What are the likely outcomes of each option?

# Vaccinations

Your veterinarian is your best guide regarding what vaccinations to give your dog and when they are needed. The initial vaccination schedule will vary depending on whether you've adopted a puppy or an adult dog and what is known about his vaccination history. You will want your dog vaccinated for commonly communicated diseases such as canine distemper, infectious canine hepatitis, and parvovirus. Do your research and follow your veterinarian's recommendations. The rabies vaccine, however, is a legal

# Car Caution

Do not leave a dog in a hot car—not even for a "minute." A hot car can become deadly for a dog in a matter of minutes. Even on a moderate 75-degree-Fahrenheit (24-degree-Celsius) day, the temperature in a car can soar, even when parked in the shade with a window open.

If you see a dog left in a car on a hot day, try to locate the owner. Note the car's make, model, color, and license plate. Ask store owners to help, or call animal control or the police for assistance.

requirement in most places in the United States. Any public office that requires your pet to be licensed will require a current rabies vaccination to license your pet. Check with your veterinarian or local authorities for your location's ordinances.

For both legal purposes and for your dog's safety, do not let your dog's rabies vaccination become overdue. Rabies is a disease that is lethal to humans and can be transmitted by any warm-blooded mammal. Many people assume that indoor dogs

cannot catch rabies, but one of the biggest problem carriers of rabies can be bats. Bats can get into nearly any home and expose you and your pets to rabies. If you find a bat in your home, having it caught and tested through a public health office is highly recommended, not only for your pet's sake but also for yours.

For all of your dog's vaccinations, your veterinarian will remind you when booster shots are due. Again, check with your veterinarian about which vaccinations are appropriate for your pet. For example, if you do not travel to tick-populated areas, your vet may not recommend the Lyme disease vaccination. If you board your dog or take him to doggy daycare, the facility may require your dog to get a *Bordetella* vaccination, which helps protects dogs from the canine disease commonly called *kennel cough*.

# DID YOU KNOW?

The signs of heatstroke include heavy panting, loss of appetite, lethargy, rapid heartbeat, lack of coordination, and vomiting. If your dog exhibits these symptoms in hot weather, call your vet immediately.

# HAPPY ENDINGS

## Sadie

While working on this book, we spent many days at the shelter. One day, Robin, a shelter volunteer, came by to say hello. We broke into smiles at the sight of the tail-wagging Dachshund trotting along with her. Robin introduced us to Sadie, who was on her way to a local TV station to be featured as "pet of the week." Sadie, age fourteen, had been dropped off in the shelter's overnight pet box with no information.

When the veterinarian first examined her, he found rotted front teeth that had to be removed and dozens of parasite bites. But, other than neglect, Sadie was healthy. I couldn't get her out of my mind.

At the time, my husband and I had an eight-year-old rescued Labrador, Kayla. Although my husband prefers large dogs, he had a beloved Dachshund in his childhood. I started talking to him about Sadie, and he agreed to go to the shelter and bring Kayla for a compatibility visit.

Sadie joined our family, and she's a very special lady. She loves everyone and is happiest on someone's lap. Her sight is failing and she sleeps a lot, but she can still run and play with toys that are bigger than she is. She brings smiles to everyone's faces!

—Jeramy

# FOR SHELTER DOGS

## Lilly

Before we met Lilly, she had worked for a living. For more than four years, Lilly earned her keep in a cage at a puppy mill, giving birth to litter after litter of puppies that were taken from her as soon as possible and sold.

We adopted Lilly from the shelter, and she was part of our family for more than eleven years. When she left us, her health had failed, but she still had the patience and good spirits that had endeared her to all who met her. Family photographs were never complete without her. She never met anyone who wasn't a friend. She wanted to be part of every gathering, even though she never had much to say. But that was another of her strengths: she was a great listener.

A two-legged friend

once told us, "Lilly won the dog lottery. Comfortable blankets and beds to lie on, plenty of toys to chew on, plenty of treats to nibble on, and someone always ready to scratch her stomach." Yet we, her human family, were enriched in ways that people who've never had a dog can't understand. We will always remember her. The house isn't the same without her.

—the Evans family

# 10 Problem Behaviors

## Barking

**Question:** Help! My dog barks all the time, and we are so tired of it. How do we stop him from barking?

**Answer:** Of course, some barking is normal. Dogs bark. Barking when a car pulls into the driveway or when an especially loud truck or motorcycle goes by is normal. Most dogs are territorial and will sound an alarm if they hear unique sounds or people come to the door. Some dogs are very stimulated by movement or motion and will bark when they see something moving. Dogs may get bored hanging out in the backyard alone or being inside all day while you are gone. Barking can be a self-rewarding behavior, just as some people talk more than others.

What becomes abnormal, obnoxious, or dangerous is when the owner has no control to stop the dog, or the dog barks for long periods of time or adds other aggressive behaviors like lunging and snapping with the barking.

Often, owners think the problem will go away on its own. The dog will grow out of it, learn a better behavior, and the owners won't have to work on the problem. That plan will not work.

What we want to do is examine the barking, try to decide what reinforcement the dog is getting from barking, and then try to change the

↑ **What's on the other side of the fence can trigger a dog's barking.**

situation to either modify or eliminate the barking. A few questions can help us decide where we should focus our efforts.

## What Is Your Dog Barking At?

Of course, he isn't really barking at everything—it just seems like it. Looking out the window and watching people walking by, children on bikes, dogs being walked, cars and motorcycles passing, or joggers going by can set your dog to barking. For most dogs, any movement is stimulating and can cause them to become interested in either chasing what is moving or insisting that it keeps moving away from their territory.

In a fenced-in backyard, a dog that runs the fences and barks at the dogs on the other side can be problematic for several reasons. While it may seem like good exercise for the dog, it raises his adrenaline level and probably his stress level. Some dogs can stay playful and friendly during fence-running, but many dogs become increasingly frustrated, both with the fences and with the other dogs. Backyard squirrels, rodents, and even birds can also stimulate barking. Almost always, barking is stimulated by motion.

# Troubleshooting

We have worked with owners who have had problems with their local animal-control agencies because neighbors have complained about their dogs' barking.

- Most animal-control agencies have specific regulations about barking, including how long it lasts.

- If you have a neighbor issue, talk to other neighbors and see if they are also frustrated. If not, explain that you are working on it and hope to improve things shortly. Thank them for their patience. Ask them to write short notes stating that the barking is not a problem for them.

- If appropriate, ask your vet for a document stating that your dog is current on vaccinations, friendly, and not a danger to anyone. A professional statement will help if you go to court.

- Work with a trainer or behavior counselor. Even if you are just starting out, ask the trainer to verify in writing that you've hired him or her to help solve a barking problem.

- Keep a journal as well as recordings of how long your dog barks when outside and at what. These are great tools to have in court.

## Reasons for Barking

**Territorial or alarm barking** is stimulated by doorbells, passersby, noises outside, and the like. What may begin as territorial or alarm barking tends to grow into bigger and more obnoxious behavior. The dog feels his actions are being reinforced because the thing he is barking at leaves (for example, the mail carrier). When you try to correct the dog by scolding him or yelling at him, he might actually think you are helping, joining in, or backing him up with the noise you are making.

Without guidance and input in the form of training, behavior modification, and even environmental modifications from you, these behaviors escalate. The dog becomes more stimulated and may even resort to biting.

**Motion barking** is stimulated by people, dogs, cars, squirrels, kids, skateboarders, bikers, and joggers—basically any creature or thing that moves. Some owners become nervous when walking their dog on leash in public because their dog barks at people,

↑ **Most types of barking are triggered by movement.**

animals, and cars. They worry that the neighbors will think they have a dangerous dog or that he is a nuisance. Often, owners will either stop walking the dog altogether, relying on the backyard for the dog's exercise, or they start walking early in the morning or late at night, trying to avoid anything that stimulates their dog to bark.

**Boredom barking** simply occurs because barking fulfills the dog's need for something to do.

## Solutions to Barking
### Behavior Modification with Training

Changing your dog's behavior starts with you. Are you accidentally rewarding the dog's behavior by your response? Phrases like "it's OK" or yelling at your dog can actually encourage barking. Even giving the dog a bone to chew on to distract him from barking at a jogger may teach him to be vigilant about joggers—not because they are dangerous, but because they bring rewards.

Instead, redirect your dog's behavior. Get your dog to come to you or at least turn his head away from the window or stimulating object. Then, when he's not barking, reward the dog. You are rewarding him for the last thing he did, which, in this case, was coming to or looking at you. The reward should at least momentarily stop the barking and give you the opportunity to redirect the dog's behavior to a toy or other activity.

If he leaves the toy to go back to barking, keep repeating your exercise by calling him or making an interesting noise. Reward his attention and redirect him to a behavior you can reward. Your dog may respond well if you walk to where he is barking (such as at the window or by the door), calmly saying "yes, I see that," and walking away while patting your leg and asking your dog to come with you.

Decide on an alternative behavior you would like to have your dog perform. If he loves toys, teach him to go get a toy with a cue like "where's your toy?" Teach the cue separately before you try using it to redirect him from the barking trigger (such as the

↑ Give the toy only when the dog stops barking so he knows he's being rewarded for keeping quiet.

doorbell). Practice in sets of ten, maybe giving a treat as well as playing with the toy with him for a few seconds.

When he is successfully getting the toy on cue at least eight out of ten times, gently and quietly have someone knock on your front door. He may start to go to the door or bark. In a happy, excited voice, say your cue phrase. Make it easy for him at first, practicing in sets of ten so you can easily keep track of his success. Very gradually increase the sound of the knock on the door. If at any point he gets too excited and barks more than two or three times, soften the sound of the knock, going back to a point where he was successful.

Plan on practicing this training over several weeks, working a few times a day or as you have the chance. If someone rings your doorbell before you've completed your training, he may regress a little, so you might direct people to a different door to enter, or even disengage your doorbell until you are ready to train with it.

If you have taught your dog to "speak" on a cue, you can add a "quiet" cue to this trick. Practice Speak but don't reward it. When your dog stops barking, even if it is just to take a breath, deliver a treat right to his mouth and use the cue "quiet" at the same time. Keep delivering treats, about one per second, as long as he is quiet. After about five treats, take a step back and say "speak" again. If he barks, that is good. Then say "quiet" and, if the dog stops barking, again deliver a treat directly to his mouth. We hope he doesn't bark with his mouth full! You have started teaching a new behavior with a cue that you can use when you need it.

A modification and training tool that can help with barking is the Gentle Leader® head collar. You can use it in the house with a leash attached. Practice using the leash and the Gentle Leader to close your dog's mouth by gently pulling straight up on the leash. His nose will go up, closing his mouth, and you have stopped the barking. As soon as the barking stops, release the pressure on the Gentle Leader and give him a treat for being quiet. The point with this technique is to stop the unwanted behavior and reward an alternative behavior. *Note:* As we mentioned previously, proper fit is essential with the Gentle Leader. Be sure to either read or watch the instructions on fit and usage.

## Troubleshooting

Acknowledging your dog's concern but quickly redirecting him to another behavior can help diffuse his reaction to things outdoors that stimulate him.

↑　**A properly fitting head collar can have many uses in training.**

## Environment and Social Stimulation

If it appears that your dog barks for his own entertainment, he is either bored or likes the sound of his own voice. You need to provide your dog with environmental and social stimulation. One suggestion is to attend a training class or a class that teaches tricks, agility, or some other fun activity. If your dog already knows some tricks, practice a bit every day. Get the kids involved. They get very creative and will love showing off the dog to their friends. Tricks like Sit Pretty, High Five, Roll Over, and Spin are quick to teach and fun for the dog. You can also use props and teach your dog to jump over a broomstick or run through a play tunnel.

Scatter your dog's food in the grass when he's outdoors to keep him occupied. Let him use his nose to hunt for his own food. Dogs love to sniff, so anything you can do to give your dog the opportunity to use his nose is great. Indoors, place several food-stuffed toys or food-puzzle toys around the house for him to find. These are mentally stimulating ways for him to get his meals.

For social stimulation, schedule play dates with other dogs that have a compatible play style; otherwise, playtime can become too stressful for your dog. If your Lab mix likes to grab collars and body-slam other dogs, don't pick a toy-sized dog as a playmate. An hour of playtime with a compatible dog can really tire out a dog. It is good for your dog mentally as well as physically because of the social aspect of playing with another dog.

Walks provide environmental stimulation, especially when you regularly vary your route. Time in the backyard doesn't really help as far as entertainment, exercise, or stimulation because most dogs know every blade of grass, bug, and rodent in their own yards.

### Changes in Environment

Along with modifying your dog's behavior, sometimes a change in his environment, such as blocking access to a door or window, can help. Drawn drapes or moving a sofa can change the environment enough to help calm your dog's behavior. Providing background noise indoors can help diffuse the noise outside.

## Barking When Alone

What if your dog starts to bark right away when you leave the house? Ignore it, if possible. You might want to set up a camera or phone to record him so you can see how long he barks after you leave. He may bark only until he can no longer hear your car, and then he will settle down to wait. If you find that he's barking longer, contact

a behavior expert to help. The barking may be a symptom of separation anxiety, or it may just be that the dog is bored and needs more entertainment when you are gone. If you normally have a TV or stereo on when you are home, leave it on when you leave. The familiar background sounds can be comforting.

No matter why your dog is barking when you're out, you should practice coming and going, using the same pattern each time. Ignore the dog or give him a treat and put him in his crate or confinement area a few minutes before you leave. While it is tempting to wait until the last second to confine your dog, that can raise his anxiety or make him try to avoid you at that time. If your dog becomes defensive, growls, or protests going into the crate, go back to crate training at a different low-stress time. Teach going into the crate for treats and food on a cue so you'll have the cue to use when you are ready to leave.

## Chewing and Destructive Behaviors

**Question:** Help! We just adopted a Labrador puppy, and he is chewing up everything he can get his teeth on. If we can't get him to stop, we will have to get rid of him.

**Answer:** Labrador puppies love to put their mouths on everything. To modify this behavior, the family will have to consider all of the puppy's needs, including exercise, safety, socialization, and training. This is true of all high-energy puppies. For some

families, this is too time-consuming and complicated, and many shelters see owners surrendering puppies at fairly young ages. Some families make it through six months, hoping that neutering/spaying will calm the puppy down. When that doesn't help, hopefully they look for options like classes and play sessions.

The truth is that all puppies will chew. It is normal teething and curious puppy behavior. If you've adopted a purebred puppy, chewing may be less of a problem, depending on the breed. But whatever type of puppy you've rescued, be ready to modify problem behaviors and prevent other problems by keeping him busy, stimulated, and engaged. If you have a devoted chewer, enrolling in puppy classes is a great idea. The first year is definitely the toughest, so getting started early and having lots of support and coaching from class instructors and other participants really helps.

When your puppy gets older, look for classes that teach agility, flyball, or another dog sport. High-energy puppies will need extra training, exercise, and mental activity to help them be calm at home. Some of these dogs also need training to teach them that they can be calm. This can be taught like a trick, rewarding the dog for lying down and being still.

All puppies will need daily exercise in the form of walks, playtime with their owners, and, ideally, playtime with both a compatible puppy and a compatible adult dog. This takes time and scheduling, but the results will be a calmer puppy who can settle down with his own toys.

Confinement training is also important. A crate is handy for confining an active puppy when you can't watch him. Another method of confinement is to use a leash to keep the puppy with you as you move around the house. You still

# Unsafe Eating Habits

We have already established that chewing is normal dog behavior. However, when your dog begins to eat nonfood items, such as clothing or rocks, this is called *pica* and can be dangerous to your pet. Dogs who eat dangerous items can damage their intestines and cause blockages that will require surgery.

Stool-eating is a type of pica called *coprophagy*. Coprophagy is a behavior that is horrifying to humans but is actually instinctive and used by mother dogs to keep the den and young pups clean by eating their waste. Young pups who've seen their mother do this may be inclined to copy the behavior, but they usually outgrow it. If it happens with your dog, here are a few things you can try.

- Check with your veterinarian for a commercial product that can be added to your dog's food to make his stool have an aversive taste.

- Sprinkle your pet's stools, as well as any other animal feces he may come in contact with, with a bitter-tasting anti-chewing product for pets.

- Keep your dog on a leash whenever he is outside so you can control where he tries to wander.

- Keep your yard free of dog and cat waste.

- Do not scold or punish your dog for this behavior. Redirect his attention to another activity where you can reward him.

need to keep an eye on him and provide safe chew toys, or he could start looking for options like nearby table legs or even your toes. Rotate your dog's toys on a daily basis to keep him interested in them, and be sure that your puppy can't chew on something that will endanger him, like electrical cords or socks.

## Chewing When Alone

Destructive behavior can happen because a dog is stressed due to lack of exercise or because he needs more entertainment when you are gone. We get calls during the winter and after rainy spells about dogs that are usually fine but have become destructive. It is a good time to be creative until you can get back to the physical exercise that keeps your dog happy and calm.

↑ **Another simple tip: If you don't want your dog to chew your shoes, put your shoes away!**

Mental exercise can be just as tiring for the dog as physical exercise, but it takes more input from the owners. Teach new tricks, hide food-stuffed toys around the house, or give him puzzle-type toys to keep him entertained. Play retrieve or another game with him for a while before you leave for the day to help tire him out. Doggy daycare is also an option.

## Inappropriate Urination

**Question:** We just adopted a dog from our local shelter, a neutered male. We brought him home, and he decided to urinate all over our house. What can we do to stop this, and why is he doing it?

**Answer:** Urine marking in dogs is frustrating. Many male dogs, neutered or not, and even female dogs, will mark. Some dogs mark new territory. If they are in their usual territory, some mark the same spots over and over. Most dogs start marking due to stress, so going into a new home can trigger it. Many dogs will mark less with supervision as they settle into their new environments. Supervision and prevention are the keys to success.

Taking nearly any male dog into someone else's home can result in a marking episode, so be very careful when visiting friends and family. Keep him on a leash for a while. Keep him away from vertical surfaces in the new location and reward him for urinating outside. Take him out a bit more often than usual to try to keep his bladder empty.

With a newly adopted male dog, watch him very closely and confine him in a crate when you can't supervise him. Dogs mark furniture, corners, doors, and other vertical surfaces, because when things smell like their scent, it makes them feel better. So some dogs, especially in new locations, are just trying to help their own anxiety. Much like house-training, we are not trying to stop the marking behavior, but we are very careful to prevent it from happening inside.

Encourage marking on your own property and discourage chronic marking when on walks. A brisk pace, a pat on your leg to get your dog's attention, and some words of encouragement to keep him moving along can help you control where the dog marks.

↑   **Owners can't eliminate marking behavior but can control where it happens.**

He can mark on your property before you leave and when you get back, but minimize marking in between.

Some dogs that have become chronic "markers" will be very reluctant to give up what has become a habit. For such a dog, doggy diapers or belly bands (stretchy fabric bands that fit around the flanks of a male dog and cover the penis) can be helpful. His attempts at marking are no longer effective, thus controlling marking indoors, making everyone feel better about giving the dog a bit of freedom around the house. The dog may gradually give up the habit of indoor marking as he starts to figure out that his marking attempts inside don't work. Consistently removing the belly band when outdoors lets the dog successfully urinate and mark outside and gives you the opportunity to reward him there.

Occasionally, there is a dog that uses feces to mark territory. You may have seen dogs who back into bushes to defecate or even drop feces occasionally while walking. Some dogs scratch the ground with their front and/or back feet after urination and defecation, apparently trying to spread their scent. It seems to be a pleasurable stretching activity for some dogs, and others seem to take it very seriously.

## Separation Anxiety

**Question:** Our dog starts to act strange when we are getting ready to leave for work. He runs from room to room, barking or whining. Normally, he's the perfect dog. What can we do to make him feel better about our leaving?

**Answer:** Not all destructive behavior done by dogs when home alone is due to separation anxiety (SA). As discussed, some dogs are bored, underexercised, or understimulated, and they find behaviors that will keep themselves occupied. Burning up excess energy by chewing, barking, or

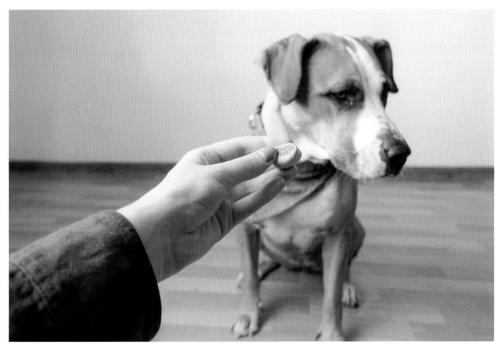

↑ **The dog may become too anxious to accept treats or eat his usual meals.**

getting into trash or closets isn't SA. Instead, SA is a huge emotional issue for dogs suffering from it and for owners who live with these dogs. Caring owners will turn their own lives upside down to accommodate and prevent emotional and physical trauma for the dog.

Some generally accepted indicators of SA include:

- Growing anxiety as the owner prepares to leave the home. This may be demonstrated by pacing, trembling, whining, barking, panting, or drooling.
- Destructive behavior, often digging or chewing woodwork around or on the door that is the usual exit.
- Not eating or playing while you are gone, even if you leave specially prepared favorites food and interesting toys.
- Urinating or defecating in the crate or in the house.
- If crated, pools of drool, damage to the crate, and potential injury to the dog, especially to his paws and teeth from trying to break out of the crate. When released from the crate, the dog is often soaked with saliva and often makes a beeline to the water dish in an effort to try to replenish his liquids.

Another trait common to some of the worst cases of SA is that the dog is amazingly well behaved when the owners are home. Perfect. Never makes a mistake, and is the sweetest, calmest, nicest dog they have ever had. He loves everyone, is obedient, and—perhaps most telling—he is always nearby. He becomes a "Velcro®" dog, one that must be touching you, lying at (or on!) your feet, or in your lap. If you move, he goes with you. He is so attentive and eager to please, yet even at this point he is probably starting to worry that you will be leaving.

SA and destructive behaviors from other causes are often mistaken for jealousy, spite, revenge, and other efforts by the dog to punish the owners. Owners might think that the dog was mad at them for leaving, so he pottied in the house or chewed up the remote control. When I talk to owners about SA, I ask them a question that can help them rethink what might be going on: "Would your dog be 'bad' on purpose?"

## Treatment Tips

There are lots of ideas, theories, medications, and herbal and holistic products that claim to help with SA, but there is no single fix. SA is a difficult behavior, and owners must educate themselves with options to try to overcome it. I recommend Patricia McConnell's book, *I'll Be Home Soon*, which is full of great suggestions for both prevention and treatment of SA.

If most owners think about it, they don't feel that their dogs would be bad on purpose, so we can go on with our conversation to find the real problem and make efforts to help.

Relapse is common and can happen if schedules change or the family moves. If the owner gives up trying to fix the problem and passes the dog on to another home, chances are good that the problem will reoccur and possibly be worsened by the changes. Relinquishing a dog with SA can be a huge trauma not only for the dog but also for his new family.

# Troubleshooting

It is not pretty when dogs panic. Sometimes it is because of thunderstorms, loud noises, or strangers. But what can be the saddest experience for owners is when their dog has a panic attack when they have left him home alone (without his human companions). Many dogs with SA live with other dogs, but their canine companions aren't comforting to them.

↑ A dog with SA may go to great lengths to try to "escape" when alone.

## Crate Caution!

If you give up one day and decide that is too much hassle to put the dog in the crate, don't expect it to be easier the next time you try. Your dog will probably think that if he protests longer or harder, you will give up again, and he will continue to escalate without some real work to change his mind. Do not give up, even for one day. You want to train the behavior of being in the crate, so you must teach him and reward him for it many, many times.

Owners who turn in a dog with SA to the shelter often casually mention that the dog does not like to be alone. They may hope that the dog will find a home where someone is available all the time, or that the dog will magically be OK in a new place. A little questioning often shows the rest of the story, and what efforts the owners tried to help the dog. Owners often struggle with SA issues for months or years. Sometimes, when we know the issues that an adopted dog had in his previous home, we can help prevent them in the next home with some instruction and tips. There is help out there!

When it comes to treating SA, working with a veterinarian with an interest in helping behavior issues is very valuable. This person can help you with potential medical issues and choosing the right medications to use along with a behavior-modification program. Following are some ideas for helping to prevent SA or working with low-level SA:

- Watch for the start of anxiety, such as when your dog knows you are leaving and starts to get worried. He may begin whining, pacing, giving anxious looks, or sometimes blocking the exit door. We want to help desensitize your exit process for the dog to help him be less anxious. Usually dogs notice when you pick up keys, put on your shoes, or anything else that means you are walking out the door. Practice doing these behaviors without actually leaving so they become less predictive or even boring to the dog.

- Never punish behaviors that occurred while you were gone. You will only make your dog more anxious about your return. Walk in calmly, no matter what has occurred. That "guilty" look your dog gets is actually an attempt to calm you down, appease you, and make you happy. Your dog does not connect your coming home with his previous behavior. He is reading your body language.

- Leave and come home in a very matter-of-fact manner. If possible, give your dog something interesting and fun ten or fifteen minutes before you leave, and slip out the door. Special treats, a treat-stuffed toy, or a chew toy that only comes out on "special occasions" can be good choices.
- Look for options for your dog, such as friends who are home during the day and can take care of him, doggy daycare, or even a dog sitter who will come to stay with the dog during the day. While that seems like an extreme option, if your dog will do thousands of dollars' worth of damage while you are gone, spending money for a pet sitter can be the economic way to go. If you are lucky enough to work in a pet-friendly office, take your dog to work. He should be friendly toward strangers and OK hanging out in your office with you.
- Leave an article of clothing that smells like you with your dog when you leave.
- Work on teaching your dog that it is OK to be separated from you when you are home. Teach the dog to sleep in his own bed instead of yours. Encourage him to cuddle when you ask him to but to go to another spot to hang out when you are busy in the kitchen.

What if your dog panics while crated and tries to break out? This usually starts immediately after you leave. If you are crating a dog with SA, he will sometimes injure himself while trying to escape by bending bars or squeezing through tiny spaces to get out. Once out, he may be OK, or he may start on another spot with more destructive behavior. Work with a professional who is experienced in SA. Your veterinarian will help you evaluate if certain drug therapies are in order.

# Puppy Nipping and Biting

**Question:** We adopted Maddie, an Australian Shepherd mix, at eleven weeks. The day we adopted her, she showed some aggressive tendencies in the visitation room, but I hoped it was just from the excitement of being out of her kennel and typical puppy stuff. I know now that it isn't. Maddie bites constantly. Some of it just seems to be gnawing on fingers and anything else she can get in her mouth, but some of it is real anger biting. She will jump and bite, too. Our family has tried multiple tactics to get her to stop, holding her to the floor to assert dominance, doing a subdued hold (like the vet does for exams), using a low growl and barking back at her, and hand feeding. Even puppy classes didn't help. We need to break her of the biting before she hurts someone.

**Answer:** The advice these owners received has not worked, and current training techniques do not advise holding her to the floor to assert dominance. It is also not

↑ **What starts as playful puppy behavior can escalate into problem if not "nipped" in the bud.**

recommended to growl or bark back at dogs or puppies to change their behavior. These outdated tactics could make Maddie become fearful of her owners. Hand feeding can often help, but unless it is used in conjunction with a training program like Nothing in Life Is Free (see Chapter 8), she could actually get worse about using her teeth, demanding food and biting to get it.

Maddie is still teething, so we can start by being certain that the toys she has are helpful to her aching gums. Because cold can help, any toys that can be frozen should be in bags in the freezer. She should have access to two or three toys each day and the rest (in the freezer) should be rotated out daily so each day she has something "new" and interesting to chew on.

No one should ever use their hands to play or wrestle with Maddie. While tug games are great for many dogs and families, until Maddie gains some control of her biting and her new teeth are all in (about six months of age), I would not recommend tugging with her.

Keep a leash on her around the house and start teaching her some self-control by tethering her to something sturdy when she is just starting to bite. Try squealing "ow" when she bites. Don't wait until it hurts. At this, some puppies will back off and be almost apologetic. If this helps, you can keep using it. If it doesn't work with your puppy, use the "time out by tethering" method. The first touch of her teeth gets her walked to her time-out spot, where you tether her and walk away. No scolding or punishment, just a couple minutes of time out.

We can teach her that using her teeth makes people leave, and other types of interaction keeps people close. There will be some repetition with this technique, so expect to repeat it occasionally for a few weeks. Maddie will quickly realize that "teeth on skin" gets her isolated.

Work with a trainer who is skilled in clicker training. Being part Australian Shepherd, Maddie is likely brilliant and probably a bit bored. Clicker training is a quick, fun way to get her working for you instead of struggling against you.

Puppy mouthing and nipping are normal; it is how humans respond that can make the difference in whether the puppy continues to do it, gets worse, or gradually gives it up. Breed tendencies can make some puppies more determined to bite or nip. For example, herding dogs, bred to move livestock for a living, can be pretty determined about using their teeth.

## Running Away

**Question:** Why do dogs run away from us?

**Answer:** The first few weeks in a new home for most puppies is spent exploring their environment, learning about their people, and getting used to their new schedules. They will usually walk or play very near their owners and might not even think about wandering away they get a little older. Then, suddenly, the rest of the world is much more interesting than the world they have been living in, and they want to head out to explore.

If a puppy or dog escapes from his home or yard, most of us will run after him, calling his name or scolding him and chasing him, which is one of his favorite games. Even young puppies can run faster than most of us, so chasing becomes futile. Finally, we catch the dog, maybe scolding him for running away. We are angry, frightened that he could have been hurt, and even disappointed that he considered running away from home.

Prevention is the best solution, so be sure that your yard is safe. Also, work on your dog's recall (teaching him to come when called) outlined in Chapter 8.

## Escaping from the Car

One scary thing that happens occasionally after an adoption is that the adopter opens his car door at home, expecting his new pet to stay put while he gets the dog's leash. Sometimes, the dog bolts out the car door and heads down the street. Traffic, strangers, other dogs, and just plain running away are so frightening to us that we automatically launch after the dog, screaming a name that he might not even know yet.

The dog may react in several ways, the best one being that he stops or comes back. Usually, however, the dog either enjoys the chase game or are actually frightened by the scary screaming person chasing after him and runs faster and farther.

Some solutions include:

- Before you open the car door, make sure the dog's leash is on and someone has a good grip on it so the dog can't bolt.
- If the dog runs out of the car, do not chase him. Instead, make a unique noise, a squeak, or a sound like a puppy or a kitten, and back up. If you happen to be able to grab a bag of treats, the noise the plastic bag makes can be very attractive to the dog. For some dogs, jingling your keys can work.
- If you have another dog, put him on leash and see if the new dog will come to him. Or the loose dog might approach another dog on the street out for a walk with his owner. Hopefully, the other dog is friendly and the other owner is polite, and you can simply apologize and thank them for helping you catch your dog.

↑ **We recommend crating your dog in the car. Put a leash on him before fully opening the crate door.**

- If you've had your dog for a while and you know that he loves car rides, call him in a normal voice, asking if he wants to go for a ride. If he knows that phrase well, you might get him to turn back. If your dog gets far enough ahead of you, use the car to follow him, getting ahead if you safely can, and then open the door and see if he will hop in.
- For a dog you've had for a while, try using other key phrases your dog might know and like, for example, "Do you want a treat?"
- If you need to, call animal control to help. They are professionals who can often help with a live trap, if necessary. If you have adopted a dog that is especially fearful, undersocialized, or even panicky, the live trap might be your best solution.

↑ Left: Your dog should not try to to go out the door without your OK. Right: Instead, teach him a Wait cue.

## Bolting Out of the House

If you have trouble with your dog bolting out a door in the house, you will want to teach a new behavior called Wait at the Door. The dog's reward for waiting at the door is to get to go through it. Work with a door that your dog wants to go through, so there is a real reward for him. It can be a door that leads to the securely fenced yard, or it can be an interior door with someone on the other side to deliver treats. Use the door to physically block the dog's way, being very careful not to let him get his nose caught as you gently shut it when he tries to go through without permission.

The goal is that your dog sits beside you until you can fully open the door. When you are ready to let him go through the door, give the verbal cue ("OK" is often used) to go through, either ahead of you or after you have already stepped through it. *Note*: Do not work on this exercise when your dog needs to go out to potty.

**Step 1:** Stand at the door he wants to exit. Stand still until he sits. While he is sitting, put your hand on the doorknob.

**Step 2:** If he stays sitting, turn the knob.

**Step 3:** While he is still sitting, start to open the door an inch (about 3 cm).

## Recall Tip

For most of our training, we end up fading, or cutting back on, the number of food rewards. With recall (Come) training, I highly recommend using treats nearly all the time for training, and use your very best treats for teaching and maintaining this behavior. On the other hand, practice no more than five times a day, so the special treats stay special.

**Step 4:** When he gets up, which he probably will, shut the door quickly. Wait him out until he sits again, and again go through the steps to open the door an inch (about 3 cm). When he can stay with the door open an inch, try two inches (5 cm), and gradually open the door more. Each time he gets up from his sitting position, shut the door. This works whether the door opens toward you or away from you, but if it opens away from you, be very careful that he doesn't push the door open.

Do not scold him and do not give him a verbal cue to sit; let him figure out that if he sits, the human will open the door. If he gets up, rushes the door, jumps on you or the door, or jumps on anything else, the door stays closed. You are literally teaching him that sitting will open the door. At some point, he might wander off, so either call him back to work with him more or just try again later.

## Escaping the Yard

If your dog has learned to escape from your fenced yard, there are a couple of things to consider.

- Is he being left in the yard too long with nothing to do?
- Is he barking and causing problems with your neighbors?
- Is he digging or getting destructive out of boredom?
- Has your dog been spayed or neutered?

Owners often tell us that the dog has plenty of space to play and lots of toys outdoors. We try to help them understand that the dog is too familiar with his own yard, he's bored with his toys, and everything on the other side of the fence is either really interesting (must go investigate) or scary (must bark at).

We want to remedy the problem of the escaping dog with two approaches: make a better fence for him, depending on whether he goes over or under, and make his own yard more interesting.

## Spay/Neuter Benefits

With dogs, the urge to mate begins at approximately six months of age. An unneutered male dog has a natural drive to seek out female dogs. Having your male dog neutered will often put a halt to his desire to escape. Females allowed to go into heat can be just as determined to find a mate, which is one reason why spaying your female is important. If she does go into heat before you have her spayed, do not let her outdoors unsupervised during this time.

### Making a Better Fence

Your neighborhood may have rules about the type of fencing you can have; however, you may able to fortify your fence without changing its look. If your dog goes under the fence, use tent stakes to pin wire fencing to the ground. You could also use woven wire to make it very difficult for your dog to dig a hole. Woven wire is thin wire, woven in a diamond-like pattern, that you can lay flat on the ground where your dog might dig. Eventually, it will be covered with grass and hidden a bit in the soil.

If your dog goes over the fence, take a look at the Coyote Roller (*www.coyoteroller. com*). While this product was originally developed to keep coyotes and other predators out of people's yards, it works very well to keep pets dogs in their yards, too. The Coyote Roller is a rolling bar that fits along the top of the fence to prevent animals from being able to get over. Some people extend the height of their fence, which can also help.

### Making the Yard More Interesting

Take all but two toys out of the yard. Every day, take two different toys outside and replace the ones that are out there, so every day he has something different to play with. Be sure to use safe, sturdy toys that he can't destroy.

Take your dog's food bowl out to the yard and scatter the food in the grass (provided you don't spray for pests or fertilize your lawn). Make it easy the first few days, gradually scattering the food a bit farther with each meal. When he has learned to use his nose to find all of the food, keep scattering it farther around the yard. He will not only have to "hunt" to find all of the pieces, but he will probably also spend a significant amount of time retracing his steps to be sure he didn't miss any.

*Note:* If you have more than one dog, feed them one at a time, or feed one inside and the other outside. Dogs can easily become competitive for food, and we do not want to start any fights.

Use food-filled toys, stuffed with his meals or treats or a combination of both, and hide them around the yard. Be sure to subtract the amount of food fed in the toys from his daily ration of food, so you don't add extra calories to his diet.

Be interactive with him in the yard. Put together a few low jumps or obstacles. Make a ramp with a board tilted onto a step and teach him to go over or through things on a cue. You can chain several obstacles together and start a mini agility course.

Get a toy tunnel made for kids and teach your dog to follow a treat through it. Dogs love tunnels once they have gone through them a couple of times. Make the tunnel as short as possible at first and then gradually lengthen it as he gains confidence. Remember, if your yard is a place where you and your dog have fun and interact, he will be less likely to go looking for adventures away from home.

↑ A safe fence should be sturdy, high, and sunk into the ground to prevent climbing over or digging under.

# Thunderstorms, Fireworks, and Other Phobias

**Question:** Our adopted dog has no fear when it comes to protecting our livestock from predators, but when a thunderstorm starts, he races for the house. Once inside, he hides behind the furnace in the basement. Is there anything we can do to help him feel better?

**Answer:** Every July, we get phone calls from owners with dogs that panic due to fireworks. Some dogs seem to do fine, but so many other dogs learn to be fearful of sudden explosive sounds that we can't help but believe some are traumatized. Other things dogs can be very fearful of include camera flashes, vacuums, motorcycles, gunshots, and thunderstorms.

Thunderstorms are a bit different than other noises because storms cause changes in the environment, making them somewhat predictable for dogs. Your dog may see the clouds coming in, feel the barometric changes, or be able to hear the thunder a long time before we can. He may start to pace, drool, try to find a place to hide, or try to break out of the house. Dogs have gone through windows and doors, escaped from

↑ Thunder, fireworks, and the like can make some dogs run for cover.

crates, crawled under beds, and hidden in showers or bathtubs.

Phobias can be inadvertently heightened by owners who are too sympathetic in their behaviors with the dog. Be nice and very matter of fact, but don't act like there is something wrong. Go about your regular business as best as you can.

Ask your veterinarian about trying melatonin. This product is sold over the counter, marketed for humans, and available anywhere that sells vitamins. There do not appear to be any side effects with dogs, and we have used it for years with fearful and stressed shelter dogs. Dogs that are having a hard time with panic often start to become calmer after just the first dose—breathing more normally, acting less frantic, and maybe even able to eat or take a treat. We have had success with dogs with storm phobias after using melatonin for a few storms in a row.

You can purchase recordings of different sounds that you can use to help desensitize your dog to noises. Start by playing the sound (such as thunder or the sound of a vacuum cleaner) very low, and if your dog doesn't seem to notice the sound, practice

Sit or other behaviors he knows well, using great treats and a happy tone of voice. Very gradually increase the volume, playing and practicing with your dog each time you do so. When your dog starts to notice the sound, see if he will keep working and overcome his concern. If at any point he becomes stressed, lower the sound level to a comfortable point and work with him

# Hannah

Hannah, a wonderful Cockapoo, was adopted from a shelter at age one. She transitioned very well into her new home, where she lived with her family from October until May of the next year. She had never been bothered by storms. After her move to a new home, however, she became very frightened of thunder and lightning. She wakes her owner up and shakes and shakes until she falls back to sleep or the storm stops. Her owners worry about what will happen if there is a storm while Hannah is home alone. She is otherwise perfectly docile and independent.

We guessed that because Hannah was adopted as a young dog before winter, she had never noticed storms before. When the summer storm season started, after she and her family had moved, she took notice. I advised her owners not to ignore Hannah, but not to baby her, either. Instead, I told them to be pretty matter-of-fact. They should bring out the good treats and ask their vet about giving melatonin, an over-the-counter product that can be useful for calming some dogs, and it can be given even after the storm starts.

It is hard to know why some dogs get scared. Even with dogs in the same home, one dog might become frightened while another will ignore the storm.

again. Use several sessions for this work, and then see if he seems more comfortable during the next storm, the next time you vacuum, or when there are fireworks.

Giving treats during a storm won't work for most dogs, but if you can distract him at the beginning of his reaction, you may be able to lessen it. If he loves toys or has a favorite food, see if you can get him interested in these things as early into the storm as possible, as this is when you might have the best chance to minimize his reaction.

Create a safe place for your dog to hide. Take note of where he goes when frightened and make sure he has access to that space.

DAP (dog-appeasing pheromone) is a calming scent for dogs that could be helpful. It comes as a spray to use as needed, in a collar that the dog wears all the time, or as a wall plug-in diffuser. The idea is to have the product floating around the dog's head so it can mimic the calming effect that his mother's pheromones had when he was young.

A ThunderShirt® is a snug-fitting fabric vest that the dog wears, almost like a baby being swaddled. The theory behind it is that the vest calms the dog's nervous system, which has a calming effect on the dog. It can also be used for other problems, such as separation anxiety, barking, travel, and other fears. The website *www.thundershirt.com* has a lot of great information.

Other ideas include acupuncture with a certified veterinary acupuncturist, homeopathic and herbal preparations, and, as a last resort, antianxiety medication prescribed by your veterinarian. If you just can't get your dog to calm down with any of the other techniques, talk to your veterinarian about the prescription medication.

# Chasing, Herding, and Jumping on Children

**Question:** We have a big fenced yard, three children, and a one-year-old rescue Collie. The kids get frustrated, because every time they start to run, wrestle, or chase a ball, the dog gets in the way, trips them, or starts barking and nipping at them. We adore Sheba, and while we know she is supposed to herd sheep, how can we keep her from chasing our kids?

**Answer:** Collies—as well as other herding breeds and herding-dog mixes—are genetically predisposed to herd sheep. So, without sheep, these dogs will then transfer their genetic drive to whatever will work, which might be their family's children. Some dogs will also herd other dogs, cats, or even leaves. While this can be a great talent for a working dog on a farm or a competitor in herding trials, it can be an annoying and even painful behavior for a pet dog.

We want to teach Sheba to channel her herding drive into other activities. Retrieving toys or balls with her can help, and she should know basic good manners like Sit, Down, and Stay. From there, the kids can teach her some fun tricks that they can show off to their friends.

When the kids want to play tag, or other games that involve running and playing in the yard, use a few of the toys Sheba loves. Put them on leashes or light ropes and have the kids drag them behind them or off to the side of where they are running. There are toys on the market, already on a pole, that are meant for this game. Sheba will likely chase the toys instead of the kids. The kids should let Sheba "catch" the toys once in a while. They will all enjoy this game much more than the one where she tries to turn them into sheep.

Another idea is to teach the children to get a special treat or chew toy for Sheba, put her in her crate, and let her have something great so they can play outdoors without

↑ **Corgis are herding dogs with an instinct to chase and nip at ankles.**

her. Don't do this all the time, but it could be a part of her day or in addition to playing with the dragged toys.

Encourage the kids to set up some obstacles in the yard and teach Sheba to go over and through them. It can be as simple as draping a tarp over a clothesline to make a tunnel and setting up some poles or broomsticks on blocks for jumps.

If she is jumping on the kids to get attention and trying to get them to run or play, teach the kids to "freeze" until she stops. Being consistent with this will help teach Sheba that jumping up doesn't work. Reward her for sitting or any other appropriate activity.

If any dog is using his teeth to get attention or seems to be escalating even with training and exercise, owners should contact a behavior professional to help work through this problem.

## Growling, Whining, and Other Verbalizations

**Question:** Our dogs, Whiskey and Bourbon, are playing—at least we think so—but our concern is the amount of growling and snarling they do with each other. They are very noisy. They stop when we call them, and there is never any injury or blood. We are concerned about the noise and worry that it will get out of hand and they will hurt each other. Should we stop them?

**Answer:** These two rescue dogs are neutered male Boxer mixes, not related but about the same age. Whiskey was adopted first, and Bourbon came a few months later. They were best buddies right away. They have been playing like this for several years, and the play sessions happen several times a day. They seldom play with toys, either separately or together. Whiskey seems to play more roughly, and sometimes Bourbon will crouch and freeze or will try to hide under a table, appearing to want to get away from Whiskey. But as soon as the owners separate them, Bourbon starts pestering Whiskey to play again. So it is possible that while Whiskey seems to be the rougher dog, Bourbon could be the instigator that actually starts the rough play.

Without actually seeing the dogs play, and with their history of noise but no injury or escalation to actual biting, we would encourage the owners to work with them on a few things.

- Interrupt the play sessions every few minutes. They are probably taking a few short breaks already, but owners do not always notice. Setting the tone for their play helps

↑　**Certain vocalizations are part of normal dog play.**

give the dogs some boundaries. When you interrupt them, call them away from each other but don't drag them apart. Reward each dog separately with a treat or good rubdown or scratch, and then let them go back to playing. Time-outs should be five to twenty seconds, very short but long enough to bring the excitement level down.

- Be sure that the dogs have other activities and that this is not their only exercise. Some activities should be done separately. Perhaps each dog gets walked by himself sometimes. We would encourage the owners to give chew toys or special treats separately, so the dogs never start to guard from each other. Playing retrieve or teaching manners or tricks should be done separately but at the same pace with each dog, if possible.

- Watch for play sessions that get especially loud, or where one dog seems to be trying to leave or hide. Do not punish the dog that appears to be the "bully," but do separate them for a few minutes. One dog may be stressed, anxious, or aroused by something else in the environment. His reaction to outside stressors can cause him to play rougher than normal.

↑  **Owner intervention can help playtime from becoming too rough.**

Quick, calm intervention by the owners can help bring both dogs back to their regular play level. Letting them work it out for themselves can sometimes cause more harm by letting the aroused dog escalate. One dog escalates, and the other dog becomes frightened. The scared dog may start to show aggressive but defensive behaviors to try to get the other to back off. Suddenly, we have a real dog fight, with two extremely aroused dogs and frightened owners who have to decide what to do. When we get to this point, it can be difficult to get the dogs to "play nice" with each other. In some cases, one dog must leave the home permanently, so prevention and supervision are very important.

The result was that these owners decided to work with both dogs separately, taking them to classes, taking them on walks, and training them separately, so that when the dogs were together, the same cue would work for both dogs. Supervised play was allowed, with a lot of interruptions. As the dogs got older and a bit less active, the play modified into a less rowdy and more acceptable form.

Some types of verbal communication between dogs can sound very serious to us, but it is actually just play for the dogs. Some dogs always play "noisy," some always play "quiet," and some will adapt their play style according to what the other dog does or prefers. It is fun watching dogs that are flexible enough to adapt their play styles to their new friends. Larger dogs can learn to play gently with puppies or small adult dogs. Tiny dogs may be able to communicate enough to be safe around large dogs, but their play should always be supervised.

## Growling

Growls can be territorial, fearful, or a warning of rough or dangerous behavior by a person or another pet. Care should be taken to determine why the dog chose to growl. Growling does not mean that the dog's next move is to bite. It is one level of communication the dog gives us.

If you hear a low, throaty growl from your dog or any dog, it is a sound to take seriously, especially if the growl is happening at the same time as a frozen body position. Our human nature tells us to punish this growl, whether it is aimed at us, another animal, or a person. If we punish this noise, we may teach the dog not to growl, but it doesn't mean that the reason for the growl is gone. Because he is still aroused or stressed, but has been taught not to growl, he may feel he has to escalate his behavior to get his point across, and that can turn into lunging, barking, snapping, snarling, and biting.

Because we don't want those behaviors, either, try to determine why the dog is growling. Is he in pain, stressed, frightened, or trapped and can't move away? Is he being "attacked" by a puppy who doesn't know any better, and he is growling to try to teach him some manners and to honor an adult dog?

If this is a stray or neighborhood dog growling at you, and you feel the hair on the back of your neck stand up, trust yourself that this is a bad situation and look for options. Usually, if you stand very still, he may sniff you, or even mark on you, but will decide you are no threat and not interesting and move on. If you move, chances are good that he will chase and possibly bite you.

Do not try to "stare down" the dog or scream and wave your arms around to get him to go away. These things will only increase the dog's agitation.

## Whining

Whining is a noise that dogs make for various reasons, but most often it is to seek attention. It starts in the nest with young puppies, as they whine and make similar sounds to encourage the mother to let them nurse. Adopted puppies often start whining at their new families to get attention for cuddle time, feeding, or playtime. If you respond to the puppy each time by talking to him, feeding him, or playing with him when he whines, you are teaching him that you will respond to his whining.

Many owners go along with this for a while, but as the puppy grows up and is jumping higher and whining louder and in a more demanding way, he must learn to use some self-control. When a behavior is attention-seeking, if we scold it or respond to it in any way (even negatively), we are reinforcing the behavior, and it will continue. Teach the puppy a different behavior, such as Sit, that will work to get attention. Sit is a behavior that the puppy can learn quickly and be rewarded for.

## Howling

Some dogs howl because of music or something they hear on TV. Some howl because of sirens, and some have been taught to howl on a cue by their owners, which usually involves the owner howling to get them started.

Some dogs, such as Siberian Huskies and Alaskan Malamutes, howl more than others. When we have a dog that howls at the shelter, you can sometimes hear whole rooms of dogs start to join in. Wolves apparently use howling as part of their communication system, but we think most dogs use it as a stress release.

## Baying

Baying is a breed-specific sound that some hounds make instead of or in addition to barking. Bloodhounds, Coonhounds, Beagles, and Basset Hounds are known to bay, and it seems that people either love it or hate it.

## "Barkless" Dogs

Some breeds of dog, such as the Basenji, are referred to as "barkless," and it does appear that they do not bark. However, they do have a huge vocabulary, including yodels, yips, whines, and howls. "Barkless" doesn't necessarily mean "quiet."

# Jumping Up

Jumping up is a greeting behavior that many dogs will use to get closer to our faces. They may also use it to get attention, as in the case of smaller dogs. Dogs will stand on their back legs with their front paws extended on your torso, or scratching at your body or arms, or wrapped around you like they are hugging you.

While jumping up is a normal greeting behavior for dogs, it should be considered a prohibited behavior unless on cue. The problem

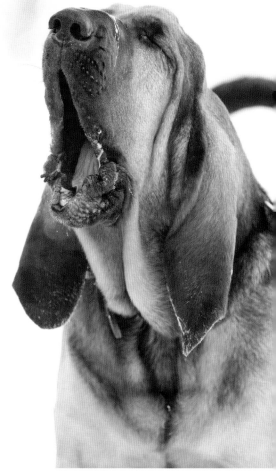

↑ **Bloodhounds are known for their distinctive baying.**

is that it can be uncomfortable, damage clothing, and cause injuries. Toenail scratches can damage skin, especially on children and older people.

As with any training or behavior modification, consistency is *vital*, and all members of the household should agree to the changes. If one member encourages the dog to jump up, the training will be inconsistent and frustrating for both dog and humans.

The same technique we use for the big dogs that jump up will work quickly and effectively for small dogs. To stop the behavior, begin by teaching the dog to sit on a hand signal or verbal cue. Use the signal *before* the dog starts to jump on you, a guest, or a stranger. Be sure everyone knows that no one talks to, pets, or makes eye contact with the dog until he sits. Proof it and practice it a lot, especially at the door where visitors enter.

You should practice when there are no visitors, and then practice when a family member enters. You may want to start with the dog on a leash so you can keep him in the area or walk away with him if he gets too excited. Finally, ask a good friend to help you change your dog's behavior and practice with that person. Be prepared to reward liberally with treats, praise, and attention from the visitor when the dog is successful.

↑　Teach your dog that there are more polite ways to get attention than jumping up.

## Jumping Up: What Not to Do

- Do not ever punish the dog for jumping on someone. Punishment can result in the dog blaming or being resentful of the person he was greeting. We want him to always enjoy greeting people. We just want him to be appropriate.

- Practice good manners when you are walking your dog. Ask him to sit to greet anyone on the walk, even if the person is just walking by. Practice this consistently so he is polite and well-mannered if someone wants to visit.

- Many people stop a dog from jumping up by holding his paws or kneeing him in the chest. These "fixes" do not work. They give the dog the attention he wants. In some cases, a knee in the chest has broken a dog's ribs. Holding a dog's paws can make him "paw shy." Modify the behavior by teaching a Sit. A dog can't jump if he is sitting.

The dog's history can make a difference, so if he was used to jumping up to greet people for years in his previous home, it could take a little more training for him to learn to change his behavior to get attention and rewards.

# Stealing and Guarding

**Question:** My adopted shelter dog, Ozzie, is part Great Pyrenees and a wonderful sweetheart giant of a dog. Lately, he has stopped eating his food and started stealing bread and other goodies from my kitchen counters.

**Answer:** This was a new behavior that coincided with his reluctance to eat his dog food. A sudden change in behavior often indicates a medical issue, so we recommended that the owner consult with her veterinarian. We also suggested she change to a brand of dog food that didn't contain grains. We suspected that Ozzie's food wasn't agreeing with him, and most dogs will quickly become reluctant to eat a food that makes them uncomfortable or nauseous. But once he stopped eating his food, he was hungry and started looking for something to eat.

Ozzie had never stolen food from the counters before, so the owner was stunned when he stole and ate an entire loaf of bread. She found a food he liked, and the counter surfing stopped. Because Ozzie just plain liked bread, she did have to be careful to keep it out of reach for a few weeks. But because he was no longer hungry, he stopped hunting.

Ozzie's owner was happy to report success with the new food. She was thrilled he loved the new food and equally thrilled he wasn't counter surfing anymore. For dogs who can't seem to break the habit, a plastic carpet runner, with the nub side up, placed on the countertops makes an unpleasant landing spot.

## Stealing

Dogs are born thieves. That is not a bad behavior; it is a genetic drive that allows dogs to survive if food is scarce. Some dogs are born polite and wouldn't take a chicken wing off your plate if you left it on the floor. Most, however, would take it without any hesitation.

Because it is such a normal behavior for dogs, we have to train them to try to keep it under our control. We also need to train ourselves and our family members to put food away, so there is less opportunity. A great training method is to teach Leave It, as described in Chapter 8, but that also means you need to be present when the temptation arises. It is unfair to expect a dog to leave a yummy opportunity if you aren't there to supervise.

↑   A big reason for counter surfing is simply that owners left food within the dog's reach.

↑ **A plastic runner with the nubs facing up will create an uncomfortable landing spot for a counter-surfer's paws.**

You can try "booby traps" for persistent counter-surfing dogs. Here's an example: put eight to ten pennies each into about a dozen empty soda cans and tape them shut. Arrange a sheet of newspaper on your dog's favorite counter and stack the cans a few inches (about 6 cm) from the edge but on the newspaper. Because your dog will put his paws on the counter first to look for goodies, he will shake the newspaper, and all of the cans will fall down, becoming an unpleasant, noisy experience for him. You can also try double-sided tape on the edge of the counter; many dogs hate the feel of it on their feet. Whatever method you try, punishing or scolding the dog is not very effective, as he will just learn to counter-surf when you are not in the room.

Prevention is the best solution. Be sure that there is nothing on the counters your dog will be interested in. This includes dirty plates, pans, or cookie sheets; any food products; and any containers or bags with food in them.

You might also want to teach your dog that he is only allowed to be in the kitchen if he is on his dog bed in the corner. Train him to that spot, using food and treats, and he should learn to stay reliably in his spot instead of underfoot after a few days.

## Guarding

An issue in many multiple-dog households is dogs that guard their food or toys from the other dogs in the family. This is a tricky behavior to change because we do not want to punish or scold the dog that guards, as it could lead to more guarding if he thinks that the other dogs got him in trouble. Instead, management is a good way to control this.

The guarding dog only gets his special treasures in his crate or in a separate room; put them away at all other times. Another option that can work for some dogs is to get several of the same toys, at least twice as many of each toy as there are dogs. It then becomes difficult for the guarder to hoard them all. Plus, they are no longer special, because there are many of them.

If your dog guards his food bowl, treats, toys, or chews from you or any human, you will need help from a behavior professional to manage and modify this behavior. Working on Leave It and Want to Trade? (see Chapter 8) will help, but more can and should be done to help the dog be as safe in your home as possible.

You can also use the food bowl to train your dog not to guard. Feed him bits of food by hand from the food bowl as you lower it. Once you put the food bowl down, though, never pick it back up. Once you give it to the dog, allow him to eat.

# Aggressive Behavior

We want to remind you that *aggressive behavior* is *behavior*. It is behavior that became part of the dog's life for some reason, and, with a rescue dog, sometimes we never know why. All behavior can change, but it will not change for the better without help from humans. Dogs don't grow out of or spontaneously recover from whatever caused them to start behaving aggressively.

Many times, we get calls at the shelter from owners who have been worried about a certain behavior for a long time—sometimes years—hoping or assuming it would get better and he would "grow out of it." Now the dog has had all that time to try to work out his own concerns, practicing aggressive behavior over and over.

Instead of waiting, owners need to get help early on if they suspect a problem. By attending basic classes with a positive trainer, the dog learns some basic behaviors, the owners learn how to teach their dog, and they all learn how to better communicate with each other.

Why do dogs use aggressive behavior? The simple reason is because it works.

Almost all aggressive behavior dogs use is based in fear. It is rare that dogs raised as

pets will fight, bite, or have any antagonistic or combative reactions that are not based in fear. Dogs learn quickly that proactive behavior, including growling, raising their hackles, showing their teeth, staring with wide eyes, barking, lunging, and biting will make a scary thing go away. It is a coping mechanism that dogs may feel forced to use when they are unable to use the "flight" part of "fight or flight," which are the generally accepted options that dogs (and animals in general) have in situations of confrontation.

A third option we sometimes see from dogs in stressful or confrontational situations is something we call *flirt*. For example, a dog meets another dog, and instead of either dog leaving or starting a confrontation, one dog finds something to play with and diverts the attention of the other dog into a game. Dogs also do this with people. If someone speaks harshly to a dog, or even if the owners are having a loud discussion, the dog may grab a toy and try to start a game. A dog can get very creative, sometimes even pretending to have a toy or just using play bows, happy faces, and submissive behaviors to interest the other dog or person in a game. For most dogs, the goal is to prevent any sort of conflict.

Some dogs have what is referred to as *global* fear, meaning that they seem to be afraid of their environment and their owners, as well as any new places or things. These dogs usually have been poorly socialized when young, and they sometimes

Reactive dogs won't be "cured," but they can be managed and their behavior modified to the point where other people may not even know there is a problem. Some dogs can be socialized and taught canine language to help them communicate with other dogs more normally.

are products of a genetic mix that may contribute to these issues.

Often, despite their owners' best efforts, these dogs live miserable, anxiety-filled lives. Sometimes, behavior modification and drug therapy can help to make them comfortable, but seldom will these dogs become "normal" dogs that are able to go out in public, meet people, and play with other dogs.

Some dogs seem to be born ready to use their teeth to get their way. We see these puppies occasionally at the shelter. If you pick up such a puppy, he growls, shows his teeth, and looks at you with a hard stare. You try to pet him, and he growls, tries to bite, squirms, struggles, and threatens. You give him a toy and start to take it away, and he threatens or attacks, ready to bite. We have seen this personality type in nearly every breed or mix. It seems to be something genetic, born into the dog, not learned. These dogs are not feral or wild, but they just don't enjoy or need human contact.

We encourage any owner with a dog who has either threatened to bite or bitten a human or another pet to find a behavior professional to try to modify the dog's behavior. Working on this by yourself is difficult and can be quite dangerous. Do not try what you may have seen on TV or what your neighbor or coworker recommends. Do not try to find a new home for a dog that threatens or bites humans or pets, as it is not fair to the next family, no matter what information you give them. It is also not fair to your dog.

If you cannot safely modify your dog's behavior, discuss your options with your veterinarian. From our point of view, if you turn this dog into an animal shelter with full disclosure of his problems, you should expect the shelter to take the responsible step of euthanizing the dog. Shelters need to make responsible decisions about the potential for damage or injury to adopters if serious behavior issues are known.

Sometimes, before we evaluate a puppy, we are amazed that he is at the shelter, so cute and young. What could have happened that the owner couldn't or wouldn't keep this puppy? When we find these threatening behaviors and can rule out that the puppy has fear, we understand completely why the average pet owner didn't keep this puppy, as the situation can be very scary.

# Fear Issues

Two main fear issues that are common topics for client consultations are dogs who are afraid of strangers and dogs who are afraid of and/or reactive to other dogs. Some dogs have both issues, and that is an especially difficult project. Each of these issues can take time, sometimes even years, to work on, depending on the owner's goals for the dog.

## Fear of Strangers

A dog who growls or displays any other aggressive behavior must have been rewarded for it, at least in the mind of the dog, or he would not continue to do it. So if the first time the dog growled at a stranger, the stranger left, the dog was rewarded. If the first time the dog barked at the letter carrier, the letter carrier left, the dog was rewarded.

If we yell at or scold the dog, he may also think we are backing him up or barking along with him. He may interpret the punishment to mean that the presence of the stranger or letter carrier causes him problems, so, yes, they are still scary. It is very easy for punishment to be misinterpreted by the dog, and it is a major reason to stop using it as a training tool.

↑  The dog backing away from the person's hand shows that he is not OK with meeting someone new.

To begin working on any behavior problem with our dogs, start with the Nothing in Life is Free protocol in Chapter 8. We want our dogs to be assured that we will make all decisions they may need, especially when the big questions come along. When you walk past someone on the street, your dog should be checking in with you, not staring the person down. When a stranger comes to your home, your dog should be responding to your cues to sit so the stranger can enter and meet the dog in a mannerly way.

If your dog is fearful of strangers that come into your home, make the decision about any interaction the dog and the stranger may have—whether your dog meets the stranger, how that meeting is handled, and where the dog will be during the visit and when the visitor is ready to leave. None of this involves punishment for the dog, and by using some of our tips, you may prevent many problems with your dog.

## Reactivity toward Other Dogs

This behavior is usually much worse on a leash than when the dog is loose. Some dogs exhibit lunging and barking at other dogs while on walks. A few dogs not only do that but might also threaten the owner out of frustration by biting the leash or

↑ **Dogs tend to greet each other more naturally when they are not on a leash.**

# DOG TAILS

## Shady

Our chocolate Labrador, Shady, came to live with us after our neighbors divorced and neither one could take her. She had run loose out in the country with their older Labrador for several years, fence-fighting with our dogs (who were safely inside our fence). I always thought if all of the dogs met outside of the fence, they would not get along because of all the years of frustration and barking at each other.

When Shady came to live with us, we first considered finding her a new home, but I quickly discovered some behaviors that concerned me enough to decide to keep her. The last thing I wanted was for Shady to get adopted, be unsuccessful in her new home, and be returned. So for a month or so, she basically lived in a separate part of our house, being able to see and sniff our dogs occasionally but not participating as a household member.

One day, my husband let her into the house while I was gone. She did fine—fine with the dogs, fine with the cats, although she gave the cats a nice warning bark if they got too close. I soon found out that with strange dogs, she was afraid and would do the same warning growl/bark. She would show her teeth and give us lots of warning, but she wanted nothing to do with playing with or being around strange dogs.

I started attending classes with Shady, teaching her to check in with me, look at the other dogs, and check back with me, and to tolerate casual contact with other dogs. She did a great job of learning the basics, had several tricks she was good at, and loved basic agility obstacles.

even the owner, struggling to get to the other dog. This can be a serious escalation of aggressive behavior and dangerous to the handler, so you should seek professional help if your dog starts redirecting his frustration on you or other people, other pets, or objects.

We always ask if the dog has any doggy buddies. Usually there are one or two dogs he will get along with. Maybe he met them when he was young, or he lives with or next to a dog that he gets along with. It is the strange dog he meets or sees on the street that causes the reaction.

Why would dogs dislike other dogs? It can start out on a walk when a large stray that rushes up to you and your dog scares you both. Now your dog fears large dogs. Maybe he meets a dog at the dog park that is brown and plays too rough. Now he doesn't like brown dogs, either. When his efforts to stay away from them don't work, he tries facing off with them, barking, and snarling. They leave. He has learned a new behavior.

From here, your dog may start to generalize that all loose dogs are scary. Eventually, all dogs, loose or on leash, are scary.

Even if we do know why the dog is reactive, the treatment will be the same. This can be a very tough process because the variety of scenarios for this behavior differs with each dog.

Success depends on the owners. Our tendency with a dog that barks, growls, or lunges at other dogs is to punish him and pull back on the leash, and we often become very tense ourselves, actually mirroring the behavior of the dog. Thus, he may think that we "agree" with him, and his behavior will often escalate if we react this way. So, part of the training is literally coaching the owner about his role—calm, quiet tone of voice; calm, but not still or frozen, body language; and, of course, steady breathing. When the dog is stressed, owners tend to stop breathing, become very still, and shout at the dog.

Punishment will not help reactive behavior. Punishing the dog for his fears makes his fears worse. Now you, as his owner, have become useless to him for backup, defense, or any other options. Do not use scolding, leash jerking, or harsh collars. Instead, train your dog for appropriate behaviors. We suggest getting a trainer with experience to help you.

If your dog has ever threatened you, bitten you, or bitten another human or pet, you must find a professional to help. It is just not safe to work with the dog on your own.

## Suggestions

The goal is for your dog to walk nicely in public on a leash when other dogs are in sight without barking or any reactions. Your dog does not have to meet any other dogs in public. If someone asks if your dog can meet theirs, and you prefer not to, just tell the person, "Thanks, but not today." You don't have to explain or defend yourself or your dog.

If someone lets his or her dog come rushing up to your dog, or a loose dog comes up, be proactive to protect your dog from having to react or deal with that dog. If you take that opportunity to step in front of your dog, blocking the other dog and keeping your dog behind you, your dog is much less likely to become combative or confrontational. You might politely ask the owner to call their dog. If the dog is loose, say, "dog, come!" in a stern voice or toss treats away from him so when he goes to sniff or eat them, you can go the other way.

You might want to carry a pop-up umbrella, so when you push the button, it becomes huge in front of you. Most dogs will back away from it. Be sure to teach your dog to be OK with the umbrella when it is open. Get him used to the noise and motion of opening it so he is not stressed when you use it. Some people carry pepper spray, but animal-control officers say that it is definitely a last resort and, too often, people end up spraying themselves or their own dogs.

## Eye Contact

Start with food and treats. We recommend not using cues at first when working on eye contact. Some dogs are great at making and holding eye contact with us, but many dogs are resistant or shy. For dogs, in dog language, staring into someone's eyes is rude and confrontational, so they may start with tiny glances or sliding their eyes back and forth, making direct eye contact tricky to catch and reward. As your timing gets better, clicker training works great for this. Start to wait a bit longer each time before you click, praise, and reward.

↑   **Use positive reinforcement to get your dog comfortable with eye contact.**

You can build up eye contact and then start to proof it by moving around the room, turning a bit away from the dog, and letting him learn to "seek" eye contact with you. If your dog is looking at your face, he is not looking at another dog or human, and two things have happened: the scary thing has disappeared out of his sight because he is looking at your eyes, and you have given him a specific rewardable job to do that makes reacting at anything else incompatible.

Practice eye contact several times every day, using food, treats, and playtime—anything you can use as a reward. You can put a cue on it. Some people use the dog's name, so when he hears his name, he knows to look into your eyes. Some people use a different cue, such as "watch," "look," or "eye." You can also use the word "here," which means you want the dog to check in, make eye contact, and wait for further instructions.

Make it easy at first. Use really good treats and practice a lot without any distractions. Once you have the eye contact game going well in the house, take it on the road. Watch your dog closely to be able to reward him when he is checking in with you. Praise and reward his checking-in behavior. The more he looks at you, the less he worries about the environment.

Enlist a friend (for dogs afraid of people) or a friend with a dog (for dogs reactive to other dogs) to help. The person should stand at a far enough distance for your dog to look at but not be alarmed by or reactive toward. We do want him to look at his environment, so when he glances at the person or person/dog team, use your cue word and then reward when he looks back at you. We don't reward the look at the scary thing; we reward the look back, when he checks in with you.

Gradually have your friend move closer, always working only to the point at which your dog starts to stress. Watch for longer stares, stiffening body, stiffening muscles, and maybe hackles coming up. If this happens, stop after one last successful check-in and work more on it later.

If you have a reactive dog, whether he is worried about people, dogs, or anything else in the environment, this exercise can help change his concerns. Too many times, we think the dog should be OK, and we leave him to walk out in front of us on walks, making his own decisions about what is scary or concerning. If we start making those

# WORKING ON WALKS

**Q:** We haven't gotten to the point in training where my dog will look back at me. He has a big lunge/bark reaction when he sees another dog, but I need to walk him for exercise and potty times. What do I do?

**A:** Make every effort to avoid putting your dog in a position where he will "blow up." Take extra-good treats with you and be prepared to change or reverse your direction if needed. Go for walks at times when others might not be as likely to be out and about. Before you leave the house, practice the eye contact exercise a few times as a warm-up and reminder to your dog. If you get surprised by meeting a dog, turn away and leave the area as calmly and quickly as you can.

decisions for him, taking that huge responsibility away from him, he will be calmer and more attentive to you, and you can both enjoy your outings.

## Head Collar, Leash, and Harness

Instead of a regular collar, use a head collar such as the Gentle Leader® for walks; refer to the product's written and/or video instructions to ensure proper fit. When working with a dog with distraction problems, keep the leash short (but not tight) so the dog stays by your side instead of a few feet (a meter or so) in front of you. We recommend a short leash on the head collar and a longer leash on the dog's regular collar or harness. There are times on your walk (for potty times or allowing him some sniffing time) when you want your dog to be able to have a little more leeway on the leash. The dog's collar should be a flat Martingale (limited-slip) or buckle collar that he can't back out of.

If you are using a harness instead of a collar, be sure it is one he can't get tangled in or get out of easily. Some harnesses clip on the dog's chest, and others clip on the dog's back or shoulders. Use one that fits, doesn't chafe or rub his armpits, and is comfortable.

## Body Wrap

Working with a reactive dog is another instance for which we recommend using a body wrap, such as a ThunderShirt® or Anxiety Wrap®. Anything you can do to help keep your dog calm is a good addition. It may seem that there are so many options for gear to use on your dog, and, for a while, you might benefit from using it all. As your training progresses, and your dog becomes calmer on walks, you can start to eliminate some of

# SPECIFIC FEARS

**Q:** My dog, Jack, usually loves my dad. The other day, my dad came over, and Jack wouldn't go near him. The only difference was that my dad was wearing a hat. What can I do so Jack isn't afraid?

**A:** Some dogs show fears of specific people, such as people wearing hats. In some cases, if the same person approaches but is not wearing a hat, the dog will be friendly. Begin to modify this behavior by showing hats to the dog. Reward the dog for exploring the first hat, then another hat, and then another, until he has examined several hats, been rewarded, and lost his anxiety over them.

Next, take a hat and wear it around the dog, praising and rewarding him when he is accepting of you wearing a hat. Once he is OK with you, move on to other familiar people who are now wearing hats. Gradually, the dog will realize that hats are not a problem, at which point you can reward him handsomely.

Be careful not to rush this training, or you might make the dog even more concerned about hats. There is a technique called *flooding*, in which the subject is overexposed to the object he fears.

If you flood a dog with a scary item, such as putting him in a room with twenty people wearing hats, you could easily damage his emotional well-being. By using desensitization—pairing the appearance of the hat with treats (classical conditioning)—you can teach the dog at his own pace to accept or even enjoy people in hats.

the items to see how it goes. You can always add equipment back in if you feel that you need it or you are going somewhere new where you or your dog might have a concern.

## Targeting

With *targeting*, you'll teach the dog to "target" something simple. For example, hold some treats in your hand and then put the treats away so that the scent of the treat is still on your hand. Let the dog sniff your open palm (made a bit more interesting by the scent), click, and reward (or just reward) for the touch.

Targeting is a great behavior to teach, and it is especially useful for fearful dogs. If the dog is so fearful that he can't touch the palm of your hand, you can try a plastic

↑ **Targeting is a simple exercise that you can start with a puppy.**

lid or even a feather. Use anything that does not scare the dog. Whatever you use, help make it interesting with a tiny bit of peanut butter, cream cheese, or other treat applied to it. After a few successful touches, take the treat out of the equation except as a reward for touching the target.

Like our other training, do not put a cue with the behavior until your dog is successful and likely to perform the task at least 80 percent of the time. It is an easy behavior to practice several times a day, but quit while the dog is successful. Targeting can be useful in further training, even obedience, agility, and trick training, so take a little time and get your dog comfortable with this exercise.

The fun part of using targeting with fearful dogs is that it gives them a job to perform for you. After your dog is proficient with targeting your hand, repeat the training with someone else with whom the dog is comfortable. Once he succeeds there, move on to someone else who he does not know as well.

*Note:* We always want the dog to perform the trick and be rewarded by *you*. Do not ask strangers to feed your fearful dog treats. It won't be effective. Even if your dog musters up the courage to snatch the treats, he is still frightened and won't have learned anything. Using a target, we can actually encourage the dog to "pretend" to be brave, doing a job you have asked for and rewarding him for that job.

You can also use targeting with dogs who are afraid of other dogs. With the trainer's social dog, ask the trainer to keep her dog busy with treats while you ask

# DOG TAILS

## Good Manners

One of our instructors, Nancy, has a neighbor, Sandy, who adopted an undersocialized rescue dog, Kira. Kira is terrified of Sandy's husband, Joe, and their teenage sons. She responds well to a visit in her yard by Nancy's dog, Rio, when the males aren't around.

Nancy took Rio to visit Kira with Joe and one of the sons, Tim, involved. Nancy gave Rio's leash and treats to Joe. Kira watched the interaction, and the whole group went for a walk. Kira was still a bit skittish but didn't try to bolt as usual. The next night, another dog came to visit, and Joe held that dog in his lap. Little successes seemed to help matters. Additionally, Nancy encouraged her neighbors to sign up for the good manners class that she was teaching at the ARL to work on getting Kira comfortable around other dogs and people.

Rehabilitation of a dog with this level of fear can take months, and family members can get frustrated when the family dog "doesn't like them." During the process, it is important to prevent any accidental punishments, such as Kira being surprised by a male's presence or being scolded by one of the males in the family. Antianxiety medications can also be helpful.

In Kira's case, it was encouraging that she seemed to be comforted by other dogs, especially when she could watch another dog get treats for interaction with people. For Kira's first night of good manners class, I suggested that her friend Rio accompany her, and that she arrive a little early to the class to get used to the environment before the other dogs and people showed up.

your dog to "target" the other dog's tail. A simple sniff is rewardable. Make it quick by rewarding your dog within one or two seconds. Gradually, many dogs build up enough confidence to be able to do a mutual sniff with the other dog. Always be the one to ask your dog to go sniff or target and then end the exercise with your reward.

Moving away from the other dog is rewarding for a fearful dog, too, so after one or more successful targets to the social dog, give your fearful dog a reward by calling him away. Be very careful not to tighten the leash or drag your dog away from the other dog. Always use a light, happy tone of voice and call your dog by whistling, making

# DOG AGGRESSION

**Q:** Our adopted dog, Olive, a two-and-a-half-year-old spayed female, is aggressive toward other dogs. Our friends found her as a stray when she was six months old. We thought she would outgrow her aggressive personality, but she hasn't. She is fine in our family and with most people, but she is terribly aggressive with other dogs. She's a 45-pound (20-kg) mix, and it appears she has some German Shepherd in her. She has not spent much time with other dogs, and when I took her to the dog park yesterday, she went snarling after almost every dog.

**A:** Olive should not go back to the dog park—possibly not ever. Taking a dog-aggressive dog to a busy dog park and expecting her to become socialized is unrealistic. Many dogs are not comfortable at dog parks. If you can find another safe, dog-free place for her to run, that would be better.

If she is afraid of dogs and has to decide on her own whether to interact, she becomes very stressed and displays behavior that makes her look aggressive. Start helping her by making decisions for her. When she can be confident that you won't let the scary dogs attack her, she can be calmer around them. You can teach her to rely on you to keep her safe around other dogs. The book *Click to Calm* by Emma Parsons is a wonderful resource; in it, she details how she helped her dog become better with other dogs.

squeaky noises, or patting your leg to encourage him to come back to you. Do not let him stay and explore the other dog or be rude or pushy. Keep control of the exercise so your dog understands his role.

With some practice, you could also teach your dog to target his own leash when he sees another dog. This turns your dog's head, which is a calming signal to the approaching dog. Often, if one dog turns his head, the other will, too, and they have successfully communicated to each other that there is no threat.

## Muzzles

We recommend teaching your dog to comfortably wear a muzzle. There may be a time when your dog is stressed or fearful in the environment and needs to wear a muzzle; for example, at the veterinarian's office so the staff and vet can examine him. If your dog hasn't been conditioned to accept a muzzle, and the veterinary staff

↑ **Condition your dog at home to accept a muzzle. There may be times, for example at your veterinarian's office, where he may need to wear one for a procedure.**

has to struggle to put one on him when he's scared, it's likely to give him a negative association with future vet visits.

If you work at home with a muzzle that fits the dog comfortably, and you desensitize him so he wears the muzzle without stress or fear, then using the muzzle at the vet's office shouldn't cause everyone's adrenaline levels to rise. Your dog will be calmer because everyone around him is calmer, and he will handle the veterinary procedures better because there is no struggle.

We recommend a basket muzzle that will allow the dog to drink, pant, and eat treats through the wire or leather mesh. Some muzzles are dangerous because they keep the dog's mouth closed tightly, and he can easily overheat.

Practice many times at home with the muzzle, feeding amazing treats and praising the dog for allowing you to put it on him and keeping it on. Teach your dog to put his face in the muzzle by luring him into it with good treats. Just like any other piece of equipment for your dog, he will do best with gentle and positive rewards during the training.

# Finding a Class and Instructor

There are several ways to find training classes that will fit your needs and that you and your dog will enjoy. Ask friends, relatives, and coworkers who have dogs about classes they have attended with their pets. Your veterinarian may host puppy classes in his or her clinic or have some recommendations. Your local animal shelter may offer classes.

We recommend auditing a class without your dog before signing up. This will give you the opportunity to see how the instructor interacts with the participants and their dogs. Look for the following:

- Is the instructor informative, answering questions and coaching participants through exercises?
- Is the location clean?
- Is the class crowded with too many people or dogs?

If the instructor is reluctant to let you audit one class, you have to wonder why. We have always encouraged anyone with concerns to audit one of our classes. Hopefully, you go home excited about training and sign up right away for the next class.

To find classes available in your area, you can also check websites like that of the Association of Pet Dog Trainers (*www.apdt.com*). The website lists members, many of whom are certified trainers. If you are in a rural or remote area, it can be much more difficult to find a class. You may need to arrange for a trainer to come to your home for instruction. For some situations, a private trainer can be ideal. If your dog has fears of new people or places, or you need to be at home for family matters, having a private trainer come at your convenience may be the way to go.

↑ **Never attend a class with a trainer who uses harsh tools, such as a prong collar.**

If you visit a class or talk to a trainer, ask him or her about preferred tools and techniques. If the trainer uses choke, pinch, or prong collars, electronic shock collars, or other harsh methods, we suggest you keep searching. You are looking for a trainer who can communicate to you and your pet without using force, loud voices, or harsh methods.

This is not a situation where "something is better than nothing." If the "something" is harsh training based on punishment, it really can make many behaviors worse. It can ruin your relationship with your dog and can actually cause your dog to use aggressive behavior because he is afraid.

# Index

# Photo Credits

Front cover and title page: Shutterstock/Mary Dimitropoulou

Back cover (top): Shutterstock/Monika Chodak

Back cover (bottom): Shutterstock/Thanat hongsamart

Back cover and "Dog Tails" sidebar graphic, pages 10, 34, 58, 63, 89, 122, 188, 205, 212: Shutterstock/ Studio Ayutaka

Sidebar graphic: Shutterstock/wow.subtropica

Author photos, pages 222–224, Kelly Kesling, Kesling Photography

Courtesy Animal Rescue League of Iowa: 5, 10, 11, 15–17, 20, 24, 26, 28, 35, 53, 54, 57, 58, 64, 66, 67, 71, 74, 79 (top), 84–86, 88, 90, 94, 98, 130–132, 134, 135, 139, 151, 153, 156, 157, 181, 182, 199

Courtesy Shutterstock: 1st gallery, 146 (bottom left); 3DMI, 215; Janice Adlam, 109; Africa Studio, 3 (bottom), 8, 108, 174; alexei_tm, 83; anetapics, 79 (bottom); Romanova Anna, 87, 113; Utekhina Anna, 195; Aquarius Studio, 148; bbernard, 33; Christine Bird, 14, 32; Aleksey Boyko, 173; Javier Brosch, 23; Christian Buch, 46; Bulltus_casso, 60; Jaromir Chalabala, 65; Chutima Chaochaiya, 29; Monika Chodak, 7; WilleeCole Photography, 123, 124, 140; Cameron Cross, 21; Daisy Daisy, 68; Natalia De, 147; Leonid and Anna Dedukh, 187; Dezy, 72; Jan Dix, 40; ELBANCO04, 39; elbud, 192; Emily on Time, 155; ESB Professional, 59 (bottom); Evdoha_spb, 201; Focus and Blur, 52 (top); Dima Oana Gabriela, 204; Glitch Visuals, 136; Andrew Glushchenko, 198; Patrick H, 186; Happy monkey, 211; hedgehog94, 4; Helioscribe, 175; Wasitt Hemwarapornchai, 171; Jennay Hitesman, 99; Thanat hongsamart, 207; Anna Hoychuk, 76 (top), 185; Philip Hunton, 63 (right); Nerman Huskic, 146 (top); Marina Ielma, 203; InBetweentheBlinks, 19, 22; savitskaya iryna, 59 (top); Eric Isselee, 49, 73, 114–115, 194; Lori Jaeski, 165; Rosa Jay, 41, 180; Tanya Kalian, 162; kejuliso, 214; Peter Kirillov, 93; James Kirkikis, 172; Grigorita Ko, 47; Vladimir Konstantinov, 146 (bottom right); Sergei Krasii, 191; Kwiatek, 96; Erik Lam, 43, 52 (bottom); Lightfield Studios, 163; Christin Lola, 145; Eddie Martinez, 30; Maxfromhell, 190; Dejan Stanic Micko, 179; Lipowski Milan, 76 (bottom); miroha141, 117; Ivan Mladenov, 121; Anna Molcharenko, 61; Christian Mueller, 107, 196; DenisNata, 142; Natalia7, 178 (bottom); Suzi Nelson, 97; Okssi, 44; Olimpic, 102; otsphoto, 167; padu_foto, 13; Martin Christopher Parker, 70; Pixel-Shot, 81, 111; David Porras, 51; pryzmat, 143; Victoria Rak, 110; Gunnar Rathbun, 126; Rohappy, 105; rokopix, 42; R-Tvist, 160; George Rudy, 89; Amber Sallot, 77; Matthew savage, 168; chanon sawangmek, 55; Susan Schmitz, 127; Nataliya Sdobnikova, 91; Annette Shaff, 63 (left); Pongsatorn Singnoy, 9; Spiky and I, 31; stall9095, 178 (top); thka, 170; Anatoly Tiplyashin, 166; Angelique van Heertum, 48; Vellicos, 78, 106; VG Foto, 82; Vivenstock, 118; VP Photo Studio, 154; wavebreakmedia, 37; Ivonne Wierink, 119; Olena Yakobchuk, 56; Julia Zavalishina, 100; Zsschreiner, 3 (top graphic)

# About the Authors

**Tom Colvin** has been instrumental in animal protection work in Iowa for close to fifty years. He began his work as a veterinary technician in Waterloo, Iowa; went on to become director of the Black Hawk Humane Society (now called Cedar Bend); and then moved to Des Moines in 1993 to become the ARL's shelter director. He was appointed executive director in 1995 and currently serves as the ARL's chief executive officer. Tom led the initiative to build a new 43,000-square-foot (4,000-sq-m) shelter, which was completed in October 2008. Additionally, Tom started a prison program, called Whinny, at Rockwell City Men's Prison, which provides extra care and rehabilitation for neglected horses that come to the ARL until they are ready for adoption.

Tom has been president of the Iowa Federation of Humane Societies since 1981, is a member of the Iowa State University External Stakeholders Advisory Group, and sits on the board of the Iowa Wildlife Center. He has also served on the Iowa Board of Veterinary Medicine. In addition, Tom was a wildlife rehabilitator and has served on Iowa deer task-force committees. He has done extensive work on animal cruelty and puppy mill investigations, working tirelessly on legislation to strengthen Iowa's animal-protection laws, for which he has received awards. Recent successes include legislation that prohibits giving pets as prizes, felony animal-fighting laws, and the 2010 passing of the Puppy Mill Bill.

**Paula Sunday** received a BS degree in zoology from Iowa State University in Ames, Iowa. She worked as a medical technician for the Cedar Bend Humane Society and then realized that she wanted to help pet owners solve issues that were causing them to place their pets in shelters. She began working at the ARL in the 1990s; there, she evaluated shelter dogs to place them in compatible homes, and she worked with ARL volunteers on programs to train and socialize shelter puppies and dogs before adoption.

During her time at the ARL, Paula started and taught the Good Manners dog and puppy training program, which included selecting and training volunteers to participate as instructors as the program expanded. After years of working with adopters and frustrated owners, she collaborated on this book, which was written to become an accompaniment to the classes and to help adopters who had questions after bringing their adopted pets home.

Paula currently owns a business that offers one-on-one, in-home training with owners and their pets.

**Mick McAuliffe** joined the ARL's staff in November 2009 as the Pet Behavior and Enrichment Manager and currently serves as Director of Animal Services. Before coming to the United States, Mick served as the Director of Animal Behavior and Training for the RSPCA Queensland, Australia, where he developed assessment, modification, and training programs for multiple species. In addition to his extensive work in canine training, Mick has applied his training skills to a variety of animals, from Sea World Australia's large marine mammals to a collection of 130 native and exotic birds, developing free-flight shows for visitors. He has lectured on animal behavior across five continents, working extensively in Australia, Japan, China, England, Saudi Arabia, and the United States.

Mick believes that pets live with us as part of our family, learning what we like and dislike through everyday life experiences rather than through strict leadership and training. He teaches using only positive-reinforcement techniques, eliminating the need for physical or verbal correction or training equipment that can cause pain or injury. He educates owners on how to teach their pets with patience and understanding, resulting in well-mannered pets and lifelong bonds. Mick and his wife, Caitlin, share their home with four cats; their dog, Lucy; and their birds, Jack and Zane. All are rescues.